Holidays with Michaels
THE ARTS AND CRAFTS STORE®

Volume I

Holidays with
Michaels
THE ARTS AND CRAFTS STORE®

Volume I

Oxmoor House®

Holidays with Michaels Volume 1
The Arts and Crafts Store®
©1999 by Oxmoor House, Inc.
Book Division of Southern Progress
  Corporation
P.O. Box 2463, Birmingham, Alabama 35201

Michaels is a registered trademark.
There may be products in the book that are
unavailable at some Michaels stores.

ISBN: 0-8487-1953-0
Library of Congress: 99-74698
Printed in the United States of America
First Printing 1999

Editor-in-Chief: Nancy Fitzpatrick Wyatt
Senior Editor, Copy and Homes:
  Olivia Kindig Wells
Senior Foods Editor: Susan Payne Stabler
Art Director: James Boone

Holidays with Michaels Volume 1
Editor: Susan Hernandez Ray
Decorating Editor: Rebecca Brennan
Product Coordinator: Lauren Caswell Brooks
Copy Editor: L. Amanda Owens
Editorial Assistants: Sally Inzer, Allison Long
Associate Art Director: Cynthia R. Cooper
Designer: Emily Albright Parrish
Senior Photographers: Jim Bathie, John O'Hagan
Photographer: Brit Huckabay
Senior Photo Stylist: Kay E. Clarke
Photo Stylist: Linda Baltzell Wright
Project Editors: Lauren Caswell Brooks,
  Adrienne Short Davis, Catherine Corbett
  Fowler, Ann Marie Harvey, L. Amanda Owens
Contributing Photo Stylists: Melanie Clark,
  Connie Formby
Illustrator: Kelly Davis
Director, Test Kitchens: Kathleen Royal Phillips
Assistant Director, Test Kitchens:
  Gayle Hays Sadler
Test Kitchens Staff: Julie Christopher; Natalie E.
  King; Rebecca Mohr; Jan A. Smith;
  Kate M. Wheeler, R.D.
Director, Production and Distribution: Phillip Lee
Associate Production Managers: Theresa L. Beste,
  Vanessa Cobbs Richardson
Production Assistant: Faye Porter Bonner

Contents

Home for the Holidays

Festive Touches

Holidays with Michaels will inspire you in endless ways to create a warm and memorable Christmas. Take a look at the following pages for ideas to fill your home with sparkling seasonal accents to begin timeless traditions this Christmas and for years to come.

Throughout the year, Michaels' buyers search for ornaments, florals, greenery, ribbons, and notions that reflect classic Christmas customs. The result is a lavish holiday collection, brimming with possibilities. With so many wonderful trimmings from which to choose, there's something to fit every taste.

All of us here at Michaels wish you a happy holiday season.

Home for the Holidays

'Tis the season to turn your house into a magical, welcoming place, filled with greenery, fruits, florals, ribbons, and—of course—glowing Christmas lights.

Warm Welcome

On a winter's night, few things are as inviting as a house decorated for Christmas.

TWINKLING ACCENTS

Drape your home with icicle lights and then punctuate it with lighted wreaths and garlands to share the spirit of the season with neighbors and passersby.

Run elegant icicle lights across the front of your house to give a bright holiday glow. Add to the splendor by hanging curtain lights from the tops of the windows. Then wrap bushes in sparkling lights.

Swag doorways, windows, gates, and railings with garlands decorated with lights and ribbons. Complete the festive look with glowing wreaths and topiaries (see pages 12 and 13).

Michaels Supplies

assorted Christmas lights:
    icicle, curtain, net,
    indoor/outdoor
wreaths
garlands
assorted ribbons

HANGING HINTS

Follow the manufacturer's instructions on the outdoor lights to determine the number of strands that can run together.

1. **To hang icicle lights,** use a staple gun to secure them to the gables. (This house has five strands of lights across the gables.) If you prefer brighter light, consider hanging a second layer of lights.

2. **To hang curtain lights,** secure them to the top of the window frame with pushpins. You can also hang curtain lights on an inside window frame.

3. **The shrubbery lights** are easy to use because they are in the shape of a net. Throw the net of lights over a shrub and adjust them to cover the shrub. (There are eight strands of lights on the shrubbery in front of this house.)

FESTIVE FRONT

A wreath on the front door signals to all that Christmas has finally arrived.

A grand wreath on your door makes a bold impact, even from the street. Wrap the wreath with lights. Then attach a multilooped bow to the wreath (see "Bows" on page 123). Wrap the ribbon tails around the wreath.

To hang the garland, hammer nails into the upper corners of the doorframe (see "Garland Measurements" on page 125). Wrap one end of a length of wire around each nail. Drape the garland as desired and hold it in place with the two lengths of wire. Decorate the garland with lights and ribbon. Place a sleigh filled with packages at the door.

Michaels Supplies

wreath
Christmas indoor/outdoor
  lights
desired ribbon
garland
paddle wire
sleigh

GLITTERING TOPIARIES ▶

Adorn topiaries that stay in planters year-round or replace them with miniature Christmas trees. Hide the bases with grapevine balls.

For each tree, wrap lights around several grapevine balls and place the balls in the planter. Continue to string the lights up the tree and then bring the lights back down to the bottom.

Michaels Supplies

Christmas tree or topiary
Christmas indoor/outdoor
  lights
grapevine balls

HOOKED ON CHRISTMAS

For a quick decoration, group ribbon-and-holly-bedecked candy canes by the steps. And don't worry about the weather—these durable canes will hold up beautifully outdoors.

Tie a bow around each candy cane. Tuck sprigs of holly into the bows. Stick the candy canes into the ground, arranging them as desired.

Michaels Supplies

assorted candy-cane yard
    decorations
desired ribbon
holly sprigs

STREET TALK

Painted signs at your front door are sure to attract holiday visitors, as well as Santa's sleigh.

The grooves on these wooden signs make them as easy to color as staying within the lines in a coloring book. Referring to the photo for inspiration, paint the signs (see right). Patio Paint ™ includes a clear protective coating that dries with some sheen. Apply a coat to any exposed wood.

WOOD WORKS
Street Signs

1. Paint the details on the wooden sign. Let dry. Paint the remainder of the sign. Let dry.

2. Use a fine paintbrush to outline the details. Let dry. Touch up with a fine paintbrush.

Michaels Supplies

wooden signs
Patio Paint™ in assorted colors
paintbrushes

MERRY MAILBOX

This slide-on mailbox cover provides an abundant greenery base for you to attach trims.

Use florist's wire to secure the flocked picks and berry sprays to the mailbox cover. Wire a multi-looped bow to the mailbox cover (see "Bows" on page 123). Arrange the ribbon tails on each side. Place the cover on the mailbox (see right).

SEE & DO
Mailbox Cover

You don't need wire or any other tools to attach this U-shaped mailbox cover. Simply pull the greenery apart as wide as you can and slide it onto the mailbox.

Michaels Supplies

florist's wire
berry sprays
flocked greenery picks
mailbox cover
desired ribbon

GATEWAY TO CHRISTMAS
Greet guests at the gate with a wreath-and-garland combo.

Gates and railings make great bases for wreaths and garlands. Accent the gate with garland. Hold it in place with wire. Attach the wreath to the center of the garland with wire. Embellish the wreath and the garland with flocked picks and berry sprays. Wire a multilooped bow to the top of the wreath (see "Bows" on page 123). Let the tails wind around the garland.

Michaels Supplies

garland
paddle wire
wreath
flocked greenery picks
berry sprays
desired ribbon

Gold & Ivory

The allure of precious metal and the purity of crisp ivory combine to create a glittering wonderland~a place where all your Christmas fantasies can come true.

METALLIC MANTEL

Poinsettia branches bundled together into a sophisticated garland give new meaning to a white Christmas.

To create a sensational garland, wire together poinsettia sprays. Drape the garland along the mantel. Tuck poinsettia sprays and berry picks into gaps in the garland. Wire a multilooped bow to each end of the garland and let the tails fall to the floor (see "Bows" on page 123).

On top of the mantel, arrange candlesticks and candles of varying heights around the garland. Tie assorted bows around the candlesticks.

Fill the stockings with poinsettias and dangle them from the mantel by ribbon. Use matching ribbon to hang a candlestick ring beside the stockings.

To make the twig tree, spray-paint the twig white. Secure the twig in a bucket with plaster. Let dry. Cover the bucket with a tree skirt. Hang white candy canes and assorted ornaments from the tree. Tie ribbon to frosted glass ornaments and pile them in a basket. Place present pillows in the corner opposite the twig tree.

Michaels Supplies

florist's wire
white poinsettias: sprays, candle ring
berry picks
assorted ribbons
candlesticks
taper candles
stockings
white spray paint
large twig with branches
bucket
plaster
white brocade tree skirt
white candy canes
assorted ornaments
gold basket
present pillows

ANGELS ABOUND

Shelves raise a collection of angels to great heights.

Place angels at varying heights on shelves and a tabletop. Surround them with beaded garlands, berry picks, and poinsettias. Put a pillar candle and holder on the tabletop. Place several votive candles and holders on the tabletop and another on the top shelf.

Michaels Supplies

assorted angel tree-toppers,
    figurines, and ornaments
assorted beaded garlands
white poinsettias
berry picks
assorted pillar and votive
    candles
assorted candleholders

PACKAGES GALORE ▶

Stack a chair with an array of present pillows and small wrapped gifts.

Tie a multilooped bow on top of each present pillow. Arrange the pillows in a chair as desired. Accent them with gold-and-ivory wrapped packages (see "Tying Tricks" at right).

Michaels Supplies

assorted ribbons
assorted present pillows
assorted wrapped packages

TYING TRICKS

1. Place ribbon on the top of the package. Flip the present over; cross and knot the ribbon.

2. Pull the ribbon around the package to the top. Tie it in a tight knot. Tie a bow.

FIVE GOLDEN RINGS

Who could guess that these charming circles are actually embellished candle rings hanging from ribbon?

Decorate the candle rings as desired with garlands, fruit picks, berry and floral sprays, and pinecones. Wire bows to the candle ring wreaths (see "Bows" on page 123). Let the ribbon tails hang from the wreath or tuck them into the wreath. Tie a desired length of ribbon to the top of each wreath for a hanger.

To create the window setting, place suction cups where desired on the window. Attach a loop of wire to each wreath to hang on a suction cup. Pin the ribbon from the top of each wreath to the top of the window frame. Crown the ribbon loops with berry sprays, if desired. Drape beaded garlands from the window frame.

Michaels Supplies

greenery candle rings
fruit picks
assorted berry and floral
  sprays
pinecones
assorted ribbons
florist's wire
suction cup hangers
assorted beaded garlands

The diverse textures of the pinecones, berry sprays, and golden fruit add to the beauty of this wreath.

ALCOVE SPLENDOR
A hutch and two small trees are decked for the holidays in the same glorious style.

To decorate the trees, place one on top of a table and the other one on the floor. Wrap each tree with lights (see "How to String Lights" on page 124) and beaded garlands. Decorate each tree with assorted gold and ivory ornaments. Fill in any empty spaces with berry and fruit picks. Top each tree with an angel and cover the bases with velvet tree skirts.

To decorate the hutch, wire together flocked swags. Place them on top of the hutch and on the shelves. Tuck white roses, berry sprays, and pinecones among the greenery. Top the greenery with beaded garlands, tassels, and angel ornaments. Place an angel on the top shelf and a cherub on the bottom shelf.

Michaels Supplies

2 small Christmas trees
Christmas lights
assorted beaded garlands
assorted ornaments
assorted berry sprays
fruit picks
angel tree-toppers
crushed velvet tree skirts
flocked swags
white roses
tassels
assorted angel ornaments
angel and cherub figurines

The wings of an angel spread over a traditional holiday symbol.

Gold beaded garland wraps the tree with seasonal sparkle.

A replica of the nativity scene is engraved on a golden ornament.

This star-shaped ornament hangs in golden splendor amid the greenery.

A lustrous beaded ball reflects the light from the tree.

An angel dressed in white sits atop a shelf on the hutch.

STARRY STAIRCASE

A gleaming garland flanked with stars lights the way for our jolly old elves, resplendent in white and gold robes.

To decorate the staircase, use wire to attach the stars at varying intervals to the lighted garland (see "Wiring it On" below). Wire multilooped bows to the garland and wind the ribbon tails around (see "Bows" on page 123). Wire the garland to the banister, letting it swag in the middle and draping one end down the newel post. Place Santas next to the staircase and on the table.

To decorate the trees, use wire to attach multilooped bows and stars to the tops of the trees. Let the ribbon tails drape down the branches. Place the trees around the Santas. Scatter beaded garlands across the floor and in the baskets. Place star-shaped boxes tied with ribbon around the beaded garlands.

To make the topiary, press the dowel into the foam ball; secure with hot glue. Place florist's foam in the bottom of the bucket. Insert the other end of the dowel into the center of the florist's foam. Wrap moss and ribbon around the dowel and hot-glue each in place. Cover the florist's foam with moss. Press floral and berry picks into the foam ball and secure with hot glue (see "Topiary Tips" at right). Attach lengths of folded ribbon to the ball with wire.

To make the wreath, curve two magnolia swags to fit the wreath and attach them with wire. Wire a bow to the top center of the wreath.

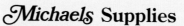 **Supplies**

lighted garland
florist's wire
gold Moravian stars
assorted ribbons
assorted Santas
assorted trees
assorted beaded garlands
star-shaped baskets and
  boxes
craft foam ball
dowel
hot-glue gun and glue sticks
florist's foam
brass bucket
moss
assorted floral and berry
  sprays
magnolia swags
pine wreath

TOPIARY TIPS
White Flower Topiary

1. Push the dowel into the foam ball. Cut the stems to within 1" on an assortment of florals. Dab each stem with hot glue and press it into the foam ball. Continue in this manner until the ball is completely covered.

2. Wrap folded ribbon lengths with wire and press them into the foam. Tie a multilooped bow to the bottom of the ball.

WIRING IT ON
Garland of Stars

1. Cut a piece of florist's wire and thread it through the hole at the top of the star.

2. Wrap the wire ends around the garland, twisting them to hold the star in place.

MIRROR THE SEASON

Let this dreamy dressing table inspire you to create festive nooks in unexpected places.

Frame a mirror with a frosted swag and anchor it with wire. Tuck pearl berry picks into the greenery. Drape tulle ribbon around the greenery. Use wire to hang an angel ornament tied with ribbon from the center of the swag.

For the dressing table, place frosted swags across the back of the table. Wire an angel ornament to each lamp. Place votive candles in holders and arrange them as desired on the table. Pile beaded garlands in a dish and scatter additional garlands around the table. Tack beaded garlands across the front of the table and attach small bows at intervals. Hang ornaments from the beaded garland.

Michaels Supplies

frosted swags
florist's wire
pearl berry sprays
tulle
assorted ribbons
assorted ornaments
votive candles and holders
assorted beaded garlands

BIRDHOUSE FAVORS

Let guests know where to perch with unique take-home presents of personalized birdhouses.

Paint each birdhouse roof antique gold. Let dry. Apply white paint to the rest of the birdhouse. Embellish each birdhouse with designs, such as dots, stars, and squiggles. Paint the desired name on each. Thread gold ribbon through each hanger. Tie a bow around each napkin, securing a birdhouse by its ribbon loop.

Michaels Supplies

small wooden birdhouses
acrylic paints: antique gold, white
fine paintbrushes
assorted ribbons

SEE & DO
Birdhouse Favors

1. Apply gold paint to the birdhouse roof with a fine paintbrush. The gold paint makes an interesting design on the textured roof.

2. The top of the birdhouse has a hanger on it that's just the right size for a small piece of ribbon.

Traditional

Red and green, snowmen and Santas, collectible villages and ornaments~these are the essentials of Christmas decorating, the customary colors you look forward to bringing out every year.

GOLDEN GATHERING

A graceful group of reindeer makes an elegant centerpiece underneath a chandelier that twinkles with sparkling stars.

Nestle glistening reindeer splendidly dressed for the holidays atop a table. Fill in around the reindeer with a flocked garland to unify the arrangement. Add color and sparkle with picks, berry sprays, ribbons, and bead garlands.

For the chandelier, wind a garland through the arms. Tuck holly garland, picks, and ribbon in the greenery. Add stars (see below).

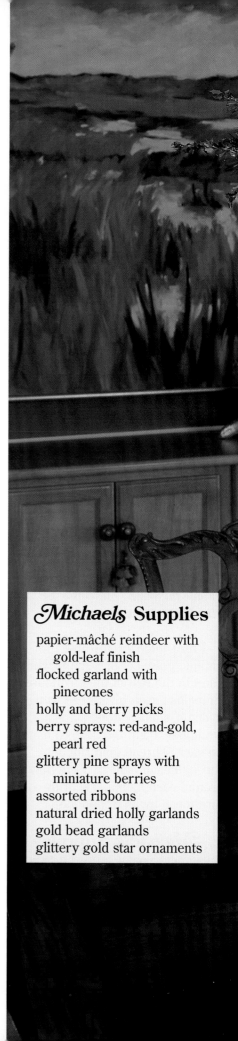

To hang the stars, loop ribbon through the top of each ornament and tie it to the chandelier.

This reindeer doubles as a floral container. Fill the opening with greenery sprays and berries.

◄ St. Nick Salute

Straight from the North Pole, this tree is covered in Santas from top to bottom.

Hang the lights on the tree (see "How to String Lights" on page 124). Drape the beaded garlands around the tree. Add the stuffed Santa garlands.

Decorate the tree with Santa ornaments. Fill in with picks and sprays. Top the tree with a multi-looped bow (see "Bows" on page 123) and arrange the tree skirt underneath.

Jolly Trio ►

Collectible Santas are perhaps the season's most coveted treasures.

Plush stuffed Santas take center stage whether displayed on a piano, a mantel, or even a chair. The Santa in the center has his own bench to sit on, and the other two fellows have flat bottoms, just right for sitting.

Santa's Day Job ►

What does Santa do in the off-season?

Well, you name it. Be it doctor, fisherman, or any number of different occupations, these adorable rotund ornaments will bring a laugh—and a personal touch—to many on your gift-giving list.

◀WINTER WONDERLAND
Create a Christmas village from a ceramic kit.

Nothing says Christmas like a snowy setting. And this one is complete with a diminutive Mr. and Mrs. Santa and their elves. To paint these houses and stores, follow the manufacturer's instructions in each kit. To set the scene on a window seat or tabletop, use quilt batting and decorative snow to hide the electrical cords and to lay a dreamy foundation for the painted ceramic houses.

TREASURED COLLECTION▶
Greenery, bright ribbon, and snow make a festive backdrop for a ceramic town ready to celebrate.

The Lemax Village® Collection of houses, people, and scenery is fun to arrange. Add to the collection year after year to create your own miniature Christmas town. Place village pieces on a tabletop with batting and decorative snow. Drape a ribbon-wrapped garland across the hutch and dot the layout with small trees.

◀TREE CHARM
Start with miniature trinkets and accumulate tiny ornaments for this Christmas tree over the years.

This fancy heirloom Christmas tree kit promises to become a cherished family memento. The tree's beaded branches are easy to assemble. Add charm ornaments, packages, and toys to the tree each year. The glass dome protects its delicate beauty.

Michaels Supplies

desired pieces from the
   Lemax Village® Collection
quilt batting
decorative snow
flocked garland with
   pinecones
burlap-wrapped trees
desired ribbon

Focus on Flocking

Crisp, snowy ribbons and brilliant white poinsettias add seasonal good looks to the flocked evergreen, creating a wintry scene that's anything but chilly!

To make the wreath, wire poinsettias to the greenery as desired. Fill in with ivy and holly picks and greenery sprays. Wire a multilooped bow to the top of the wreath and let the tails hang (see "Bows" on page 123).

To make each swag, wire poinsettias to the greenery as desired. Fill in with ivy and holly picks and greenery sprays. Wire a mulitlooped bow to the top of the swag and let the tails fall. Place the suction cup hanger on the window and attach the swag with wire.

Michaels Supplies

flocked wreath with
  pinecones
florist's wire
picks: poinsettia, ivy, holly
greenery sprays with white
  berries
desired ribbon
flocked swags
suction cup hangers

BANISTER HIGHLIGHTS

A tumbling garland wrapped with red ribbon and bedecked with oversize ornaments sets the stage for this joyous season.

Wind the greenery around the stairway railing. Wire the ornaments to the garland. Wire a mulitlooped bow to the bottom of the banister and let the tails hang (see "Bows" on page 123). Starting at the bow, wrap a length of ribbon around the garland.

Michaels Supplies

flocked garland with
   pinecones
florist's wire
assorted large ornaments
desired ribbon

Festive Fireside

A bright mantel scarf provides the backdrop for a spirited gathering of characters.

To make the mantel scarf, cut fringe along two adjacent edges of the felt rectangles. The number of rectangles that you need will depend on the mantel's length. (This mantel has 17 rectangles.) Cut an assortment of felt star shapes. Glue buttons to the stars. Glue stars to the rectangles and line them across the mantel.

To make the felt trees, for each large tree, cut 1 (14" x 19") felt strip; then cut 7 (6"-wide) strips in each of the following lengths: 19", 16", 14", 12", 10", 8", and 6". Cut a 7½" felt circle. For the small tree, cut 1 (3" x 17") felt strip; then cut 7 (4½"-wide) strips in the following lengths: 17", 14", 12", 11", 9", 8", and 6". Cut a 6½" felt circle. Cut fringe along the bottom edge of each 6"- and 4½"-wide felt strip.

For each large tree, mark a line on the foam 5" from the bottom; then mark lines at 3" increments up to the top of the tree. Glue the 4" x 9" strip to the bottom of the tree. For the small tree, mark a line on the foam 4" from the bottom and then mark lines at 2¼" increments up to the top of the tree. Glue the 3" x 17" strip to the bottom of the tree.

Glue the fringe strips along the tree form (see "Tiny Tree Tips" at right). When the tree is covered, center the felt circle on top of the tree and glue it in place. Let dry. Trim the tree as desired.

To make the tree skirt, trim the edges of one red felt square to form a 36" circle. Cut a 20" circle from the remaining red felt square. Cut a 6" circle in the center of the smaller red circle. Cut a 24" circle from the green felt square. Cut fringe along the outer edges of the felt circles.

Center and stack the felt circles, from the largest to smallest circle. Cut through all layers from the outer edge to the center to make a slit for the skirt. Cut out the center of the medium and large circles to match the hole in the small circle. Glue the layers together. From the felt remnants, cut an assortment of star shapes. Glue buttons to the stars. Glue the stars to the skirt as desired. Apply Velcro dot fasteners to the skirt's slit to close.

To put it together, top the mantel scarf with the felt trees, beaded garlands, and greenery. Decorate the miniature trees with lights and garlands; place the skirt underneath them. Arrange the bears and the sleighs opposite the trees.

Michaels Supplies

felt mantel scarf (See below.)
felt trees (See below.)
felt tree skirt (See below.)
snowmen
assorted beaded garlands
flocked pine floral sprays
berry floral sprays
3 miniature trees
Christmas lights
star minigarland
miniature sleighs
assorted bears
For the mantel scarf:
felt rectangles: red, green
craft glue
craft buttons
For the felt trees:
craft foam trees: 2 (24"),
    1 (18")
2 sheets 36" square green felt
⅜" gold wire ribbon
wired gold bead trim
decorative red birds
miniature birdhouse ornaments
straight pins
low-temperature glue gun and
    glue sticks
For the felt tree skirt:
36" squares felt: 2 red,
    1 green
craft buttons: red, yellow
craft glue
Velcro® dot fasteners

TINY TREE TIPS
Fringed Felt

1. For each tree, align the longest fringe strip along the bottom mark on the tree form, overlapping it slightly and pinning it in place around the tree. Glue it in place and remove the pins. Repeat with the other fringed strips, working from longest to shortest.

2. Wrap the tree with mini-garlands. Glue or pin ornaments and birdhouses to the tree as desired. Use the wire attached to the birds to hold them in place. To make the tree topper, bend the wired gold beaded trim into the shape of a star. Pin the star and a bird to the top of the tree.

Michaels Supplies

greenery centerpiece
assorted ribbons
assorted taper and votive
    candles
votive holders
topiaries in clay pots
berry floral picks and sprays
evergreen wreaths
glittered ivy picks

◀ SET FOR ENTERTAINING

Instead of placing a party favor in front of each guest's place, attach an unexpected wreath to the back of each chair.

For the table, arrange the greenery centerpiece as desired. Add ribbons, candles in holders, and berry picks. Embellish the topiaries with ribbons and picks and place one on each side of the candle arrangement.

For the chairs, embellish the garland wreaths with picks (see "Charming Chairbacks" below). Top the wreaths with bows and tie them to the chairbacks.

CHARMING CHAIRBACKS

Cut a garland into small lengths to customize a wreath to fit your chair. Shape the garland into a circle and wire the ends together. Use the ribbon at the top to hide the wire.

CHRISTMAS BIRDHOUSES

Nest these enchanted birdhouses on a sideboard.

Arrange the birdhouses as desired. Surround them with greenery, beaded garlands, grapevine, and pinecones for an outdoorsy tablescape.

To make the wreath, tuck the birdhouse picks into the greenery. Wrap the wreath with grapevine. Tie a multi-looped bow and wire it to the wreath as desired (see "Bows" on page 123).

Michaels Supplies

assorted painted wooden
  birdhouses
mixed greenery floral picks
assorted beaded garlands
grapevine wreath (unwound)
flocked red pinecones
flocked wreath
wooden birdhouse picks
desired ribbon

Della Robbia

Revel in the sumptuous style influenced by the fifteenth~century Florentine sculptor Andrea della Robbia, who laced his works with garlands of fruit.

BOUNTIFUL BUFFET

Frame an inviting setting with generous helpings of fruits and ribbons.

To create a Della Robbia garland, wire together the fruit sprays. Attach the garland where desired, letting the center swag. Tie a multilooped bow and wire it to one corner (see "Bows" on page 123). Trail ribbon tails through the garland.

To make the fruited topiary, place a topiary form in the center of your chosen urn or container. Hot-glue the fruits as desired around the form (see "Topiary Tips" below). Fill in any gaps with moss.

To make each candle ring, place a candle wreath at the top of a candlestick. Wire the fruits around the wreath. Then place a candle in the center of the arrangement.

To complete the arrangement, place fruit as desired atop the buffet table. Wire fruits and greenery to a bottle of sparkling water.

Michaels Supplies

Assorted Della Robbia decorations: fruit sprays, fruits, candle wreaths
florist's wire
assorted ribbons
topiary form
hot-glue gun and glue sticks
moss
pillar candles

TOPIARY TIPS
Fruited Tree

1. Starting at the base of the tree, glue grapes to the cone.

2. Continue around and up the cone with assorted large and small fruit (see the photos).

MAGICAL MANTEL

Holiday greenery, luscious fruits, strings of cranberries, and grapevine balls make a handsome setting for a collection of Santas.

To set the stage for this dramatic scene, trail a garland across the mantel and let the ends fall to the floor. Wire fruits to the greenery or tie with ribbon. To add height and interest, arrange Santas across the mantel. Elevate some by placing them on top of books tucked under the greenery.

In front of the fireplace, arrange the trees as desired. Tie multilooped bows to the tops of the trees (see "Bows" on page 123). Swirl cranberry garlands around the bottom of the trees. Add a large Santa.

Wrap the grapevine balls with ribbons. Place them amidst the cranberry garlands and where desired on the mantel.

Michaels Supplies

garland
florist's wire
assorted fruits
assorted Santas
Alpine trees
assorted ribbons
cranberry garlands
grapevine balls

TERRA-COTTA TREES

Plain pots assume a glamorous identity when painted and stacked upside down. Top these tiny trees with ribbons and fruits.

For each tree, paint the pots in the desired color. Let dry. Insert florist's foam into each pot. Stack the pots (see "See & Do" below). Top the tree with a multilooped bow and then tuck a berry pick into the bow.

To create the tablescape, place a tree skirt on a table. Cover the tree skirt with moss. Nestle an array of trees in the moss. Cut a grapevine wreath and wind it around the setting. Arrange the garlands, the remaining picks, and assorted ribbons and balls around the trees.

Michaels Supplies

terra-cotta pots in graduated sizes
    for each tree
paints: gold, copper, silver
paintbrushes
florist's foam
dowel
assorted ribbons
tree skirt
moss
grapevine wreath
assorted beaded garlands
berry picks
beaded and moss balls

SEE & DO
Stacked Tree

1. Insert a dowel through the hole in the bottom of the first pot.

2. Stack the remaining pots on top of each other through the dowel.

TRIO OF TREES

Adorn clustered trees with sparkling fruits, swags, and ornaments in rich jewel tones to brighten any holiday home.

For any tree, the first step in decorating is to put on the lights (see "How to String Lights" on page 124).

Then wrap the garlands or add ribbon. The small red tree (at right) is encircled with cranberry garlands; the copper-and-gold tree (at left) features beaded garlands with tassels. The burgundy tree (in the center) sports gold-trimmed ribbon wired to the tips of the branches.

Add fruit ornaments, fruit picks, and bird's nests. For the grand finale, top each tree with an angel.

Michaels Supplies

Christmas trees
Christmas lights
assorted cranberry and
    beaded garlands
assorted ribbons
bird's nest ornaments
Della Robbia decorations:
    fruit picks, ornaments
angel tree-toppers
assorted baskets

Ornaments, such as this Santa, make standout package-toppers.

Michaels Supplies

garland
florist's wire
hot-glue gun and glue sticks
berry and fruit picks
gold ball ornaments
desired ribbon
long florist's sticks
pillar candles
hurricane globes
candle rings

◀ FRUITFUL ENDEAVORS

Celebrate Christmas in all corners of your house with such festive accents as greenery swagged around a frame.

To assemble the garland, wire the fruits and the balls around the garland. Hot-glue the berry picks, the fruit picks, and the gold balls where desired on the garland. Tie a multilooped bow, leaving long tails (see "Bows" on page 123). Wire the bow to the garland and trail the tails through the garland. Attach the garland to the frame (see "Hidden Support" below).

For the candle arrangement, place candles and hurricane globes inside the candle rings. Press berry and fruit picks into the rings. Wrap ribbon around the arrangement.

HIDDEN SUPPORT
Garland

To hold the garland in place, wedge long florist's sticks from in front of the garland to behind the picture frame until the garland is secure. Fluff the garland to hide the sticks.

GLASS MENAGERIE
Pile ornaments in bowls and glasses for a showstopper you create in a snap.

For the tabletop, fill the bowls, the cake plates, and the glasses with colorful ornaments that provide a sparkle that guests can't miss. Tie some with ribbon and wrap the remaining ribbon around the arrangement. Place small berry picks amongst the ribbon. Situate a candle ring beside the glass arrangement and complete the lavish look with a votive candle inside a brandy snifter or a glass holder.

For the backdrop, place a candle ring on top of a candelabra or other fixture and embellish it with ribbon and ornaments.

Michaels Supplies

assorted glass containers
assorted glass fruit ornaments
assorted ribbons
berry picks
candle rings
votive candles and holders

HUNG WITH CARE

The family stockings wait fireside for jolly Saint Nick.

To help Santa out, fashion a name tag for each stocking with decorative paper and ribbon. For a quick arrangement, place apple branches on the mantel. Then intersperse candles in holders. Add a ribbon-and-garland flourish.

Attach name tags to personalize Della Robbia stockings.

DIAMOND RINGS

Gold fruits, cherubs, and ribbon shine amid smaller Della Robbia fruits and berries in pine wreaths.

These diamond-shaped wreaths provide a festive twist on the traditional rounds. For each wreath, place picks as desired around the wreath. Then hot-glue cherubs and bird's nests to the wreath. Tie a multilooped bow wreath and wire it where desired (see "Bows" on page 123). Wrap the ribbon tails around the wreath.

Michaels Supplies

diamond-shaped pine wreaths
Della Robbia fruit picks
gold fruit and berry picks
hot-glue gun and glue sticks
gold cherubs
gold bird's nest ornaments
desired ribbon
florist's wire

SEASONAL SWAG
The light reflected from a gold sconce makes Christmas decorations gleam.

A greenery badge accentuates a sconce but does not overpower the fixture. Wire the fruit branch to the greenery and then wire the greenery to the sconce. Wrap ivy rings around the candlesticks. Wire a multilooped bow to the sconce (see "Bows" on page 123).

Michaels Supplies

florist's wire
fruit branch
greenery badge
ivy
desired ribbon

Victorian

Celebrate the season by stepping back in time to an age of elegance and romance.

MANTEL FLOURISH

A fireplace topped with a fanciful garland, ribbons, florals, and rich-colored ornaments makes a handsome living room focal point.

Rest a garland on the mantel and let it cascade down the sides (see "Garland Measurements" on page 125). Stick greenery picks in the garland for extra fullness. Wire ornaments and cherubs to the greenery and let some hang in front of the mantel. Wire bows to the garland and wind the tails around the garland (see "Bows" on page 123).

Fill the stockings with rose and berry picks. Hang them at various lengths with ribbon. Wire a multi-looped bow to the top of each stocking.

For the topiaries on top of the mantel, paint the terra-cotta pots gold and antique gold. Let dry. Arrange the topiaries on the mantel, placing some on books to vary the heights. Top some of the topiaries with snowflake picks.

Michaels Supplies

sparkling garland
greenery picks
florist's wire
ornaments
gold cherubs
assorted ribbons
stockings
floral and berry picks
Patio Paints™: gold, antique
   gold
paintbrushes
topiaries in terra-cotta pots
gold snowflake picks

BRILLIANT BRANCHES

Make a delicate yet bountiful impression with richly varied Victorian ornaments.

Before you decorate the tree, string the lights (see "How to String Lights" on page 124). Wrap the burgundy and gold beaded garlands around the tree for a rich appearance.

Combine the florals and the ornaments for a luscious look. Generously cover the tree with lots of flocked poinsettias and dainty beaded ornaments. Hang some of the ornaments on the tree with narrow pink and white ribbons. Fill in empty spaces with frosted balls. Top the tree with an exquisite Victorian angel.

Michaels Supplies

Christmas tree
Christmas lights
frosted, decorative, and
    beaded balls
Victorian ornaments
burgundy and gold garlands
berry picks
angels
flocked poinsettias
angel tree-topper

Tiny ribbon roses give depth to a Christmas shoe.

An angel exudes peace from atop the Christmas tree.

Trims and ribbons quaintly embellish a heart-shaped ornament.

Textured Christmas bells ring in the season of joy.

Tie ornaments to the tree with ribbon to give them even more appeal.

Wrapped packages add to the suspense and excitement of Christmas.

Michaels Supplies

flocked wreath
assorted ribbons
florist's wire
gold cherubs
hydrangea picks
tassel ornaments
greenery sprigs

◀ ARTFUL ENTRY

Dress up a mirror for the holidays with a spectacularly embellished wreath.

To make the wreath, hold two lengths of different ribbon together to make a multilooped bow (see "Bows" on page 123). Wire the bow to the top of the wreath. Wind the tails through the greenery. Attach the cherubs to the wreath with wire as desired. Intersperse hydrangea picks in the wreath. Wire tassel ornaments to the wreath to fill in any gaps.

Below the wreath, ring candelabra tapers with greenery sprigs. Tie tassel ornaments to each holder with narrow ribbon. Set bow-topped tassel ornaments on the table.

HYDRANGEA KISSING BALL ▶

Who needs mistletoe when you can greet guests with a foam ball covered with hydrangea?

Hot-glue hydrangea picks to a foam ball. Holding the lengths together, tie two colors of ribbon in a multilooped bow, leaving long tails. Pin the bow to the bottom of the ball. Then tie another multilooped bow with two lengths of one color of ribbon, leaving long tails. Pin the solid bow to the top of the ball and tie the ribbon tails to a light fixture.

Michaels Supplies

hot-glue gun and glue sticks
hydrangea picks
craft foam ball
assorted ribbons
florist's pins

PRETTY IN PINK
Decorate a wreath for a headboard and a small tree for a side table with poinsettias, ornaments, and ribbon.

Cover the wreath with poinsettias. Fill in with snowflakes and berry sprays. Wire crocheted ornaments to the wreath as desired. Attach a multi-looped bow to the top of the wreath (see "Bows" on page 123). Let the ribbon tails fall. Cluster crochet reindeer around the bow. Tie the wreath to the headboard with a loop of ribbon.

Place the small tree on a table or a chest. String on the lights (see "How to String Lights" on page 124) and the garlands. Decorate the tree with the ornaments and the florals. Crown the tree with the Santa tree-topper. Drape a tree skirt over the base of the tree. Scatter loose poinsettias on the skirt.

Michaels Supplies

wreath
pink and white poinsettias
white snowflake picks
miniature white berry sprays
crochet ornaments:
    assorted, reindeer
florist's wire
assorted ribbons
assorted garlands
frosted clear balls
Santa tree-topper
gold-and-white tree skirt

GRACEFUL GLOW

In the intimate space of a bathroom, this celestial setting, abundant with aromatic candles, provides a heavenly experience.

Place angels as desired on a tabletop or a counter. Use the height, the colors, and the sizes of the angels as guides for the rest of the decoration. To create a backdrop, hang star ornaments by ribbon from suction cups on a mirror, a shower door, or a window. Fill existing containers with florals and candy canes, as we did with the porcelain pitcher and the glass jars. Add more florals to crocheted baskets. Arrange pillar and votive candles in holders as desired. Tie ribbon around the pillar candles and stick elegant rose picks in the bows.

Michaels Supplies

assorted porcelain angels
assorted ornaments
assorted ribbons
suction cup hangers
rose picks
white candy canes
white crocheted baskets
miniature berry sprays
poinsettia picks
pillar and votive candles
votive and pillar holders

Michaels Supplies

sprays: poinsettias,
   hydrangeas, berries,
   roses
glittering garland
glittering wreath
florist's picks
assorted ribbons
greenery picks
pinecones
pillar and votive candles
glass candleholders
burlap-wrapped tree
beaded garland

◀ GRAND HUTCH

Don't forget to decorate the place where friends and family love to congregate: the kitchen.

For the top of the hutch, cut poinsettias from their stems and arrange them around a garland and a wreath, securing them with florist's picks (see "Poinsettia Pointer" below and "Garland Measurements" on page 125). Add hydrangeas and roses in the same manner. Tuck in berry sprays, separating the clusters for fuller berries. Wire a multilooped bow to the wreath and let the tails fall (see "Bows" on page 123). Drape the garland over the top of the hutch. Center the wreath on the garland.

On the shelves of the hutch, display your china, whether the colors are Christmassy or not. Place greenery picks around the china. Include floral and berry sprays amidst the greenery. Add pinecones and votive candles in holders.

On the tabletop of the hutch, group varying heights of pillar candles. Decorate a small tree with a beaded garland, berry picks, and ribbon.

POINSETTIA POINTER

Use clippers to cut the poinsettia flowers from their stems, which makes them easier to use on garlands and wreaths. Leave enough of the stem to wrap the wire of a florist's pick around it and to press it into the greenery.

LINENS AND LACE

Surprise guests with a tiny Victorian tree in your powder room.

String the tree with a small strand of lights. Encircle the tree with a minigarland. Tie narrow ribbon on the branches. Hang the ornaments on the tree. Place an opened parasol ornament on top of the tree. Tie a bow around the burlap base of the tree.

Michaels Supplies

mini tree
Christmas lights
beaded minigarland
assorted ribbons
Victorian ornaments

SEASONAL NOOK

A favorite piece of furniture becomes an angelic setting when accented with Christmas florals and topped with a ribbon wreath.

To make the ribbon wreath, wrap the form with ribbon (see "See & Do" below). Enhance the wreath with a multilooped bow, a cherub, floral picks, and berry sprays. Hang the wreath above the desk.

Top the desk with greenery picks to create a minigarland. Wire florals and ribbon in place as desired. Arrange pillar candles amidst the greenery.

On the desk surface, set an angel in the nook. Place candleholders with attached greenery as desired. Use florist's wire to attach the ribbon, the cherubs, and the florals to the greenery. Put the tapers into the candleholders.

Michaels Supplies

craft foam wreath form
desired ribbon
glue or straight pins
florist's wire
assorted gold cherubs
magnolia sprays
berry sprays
greenery picks
porcelain angel
candleholders with greenery
pillar and taper candles

SEE & DO
Ribbon Wreath

1. Wrap the wreath form tightly with 1"- to 2"-wide ribbon, overlapping the ribbon slightly.

2. Secure the ribbon at the back of the wreath with glue or with straight pins.

DOLLHOUSE ORNAMENT TREE

Enchant a child with a tree just her size, decorated with tiny furniture ornaments.

Before you decorate the tree, wrap it with lights (see "How to String Lights" on page 124). Then string the garlands around the tree.

Hang the ornaments on the tree with narrow ribbon loops. Use wider ribbon to tie bows on some branches. Secure heavy ornaments to the limbs with florist's wire. Tuck in light pink poinsettia, rose, and berry picks on the tree. Set some furniture ornaments on the floor in front of the tree. Wire a multilooped bow to the top of the tree (see "Bows" on page 123).

Michaels Supplies

Christmas tree
Christmas lights
assorted beaded garlands
assorted ornaments
assorted ribbons
florist's wire
picks: berries, roses,
   poinsettias

Festive Touches

It's the little traditions that make Christmas so enchanting. Welcome the season with such joys as favorite recipes, glowing candles, and handmade ornaments. Spread your cheer with handcrafted greeting cards, gifts wrapped with style, and thoughtfully framed family photographs.

Creative Cards

Keep in touch with friends and family by sending greetings fashioned by you.

CANDY-CANE CARD

A stamped image set off by red vellum achieves a stained-glass look.

Cut and fold the card stock to the desired size. Stamp the candy canes on the front of the card. Use the red pen to color the candy-cane stripes, the green pen to color the holly leaves, and the gold opaque pen to color the ribbon. Referring to the photo, with card open and flat cut out a window around the candy canes. Line the inside front of the card with vellum behind the cutout window. Draw a red border around the card.

Michaels Supplies

white card stock
craft knife
candy-cane stamp
green ink pad
permanent markers: red, green, gold opaque
red vellum

ALL THAT GLITTERS

Handmade paper and embossing tools add sparkle to a stamped-on Christmas tree.

1. Cut and fold the card stock to the desired size. Cut a window in the center of the card front.

2. Referring to the photo, use the glue pen to draw a border around the window. Sprinkle silver embossing powder onto the glue border. Following the manufacturer's instructions, use the heat tool to emboss the border.

3. Stamp the tree onto the handmade paper. Sprinkle it with gold embossing powder. Emboss it with the heat tool.

4. Center the embossed tree in the window. Cover the inside of the card with white paper. Write a message as desired.

Michaels Supplies

white card stock
craft knife
glue pen
embossing powder: silver, gold
heat tool
tree stamp
green ink pad
white handmade paper
black fine-tip permanent
   marker
white paper

LAYERED LOOK

A row of rub-on transfer trees gives a touch of whimsy to this greeting.

1. Cut and fold the red card stock to the desired size, trimming 1 long edge 1" shorter than the other. Cut a piece of vellum ¼" shorter than the short card front. Cut a piece of white stock ¼" longer than the short front.

2. Referring to the photo, apply the transfers to the vellum. Punch stars above the trees. Cut a decorative border along the base of the trees.

3. Cover the red card with the vellum. Referring to the photo, cut slits across the front of the vellum and the red card. Run ribbon through the slits and tie a bow. Tape the ribbon ends to the inside front of the card.

4. Trim the white card stock with the decorative-edge scissors. Glue it inside the card. Draw red dots across the white border.

Michaels Supplies

card stock: red, white
clear striped vellum
craft knife
tree rub-on transfers
star punch
desired ribbon
decorative-edge scissors
red fine-tip permanent marker

SANTA CLAUS IS COMING

Wish friends a happy holiday season with this jolly card.

1. Cut and fold the red card stock to the desired size. Glue the handmade paper to the center of the red card.

2. Use the glue pen to draw a border around the handmade paper. Sprinkle gold embossing powder on the glue. Shake off any excess. Following the manufacturer's instructions, use the heat tool to set the embossing powder.

3. Apply the Santa rubber stamp to the white card stock. Color Santa with the opaque pens. Embellish Santa with embossing powder and emboss with the heat tool. Cut out and center Santa on the handmade paper.

Michaels Supplies

card stock: red, white
red handmade paper
glue pen
gold embossing powder
heat tool
Santa rubber stamp
opaque pens in desired colors

EMBOSSED GIFT TAG

Here's a quick way to make a great-looking label for a holiday gift.

1. Stamp "to" and "from" onto a tag.

2. Sprinkle embossing powder onto the images. Shake off the excess powder.

3. Emboss the images with the heat tool.

4. Write the desired names on the tag with the markers.

Michaels Supplies

rubber stamps: "to," "from"
ink pad in desired color
price tag
embossing powder
heat tool
fine-tip markers: green, red

ORNAMENT CARDS

Preserve each favorite holiday greeting by turning it into an ornament.

For each, cover the card with laminate. Punch holes in the top of the card. Thread the ribbon through the holes; tie to make a hanger.

Michaels Supplies

Christmas photo cards
Keep a Memory Self-
   Adhesive Laminate
hole punch
assorted ribbons

Happy holidays from Virginia!

Peace on Earth
1998

JUD, COURTNEY
AND MOSES

WOVEN TREE

Opening a card decorated with ribbon is almost as much fun as unwrapping a Christmas package.

1. Cut and fold the red card stock into the desired size. Draw a tall triangle on the card front. Cut 14 slits around the triangle: 5 on the base, 4 on the left side, and 5 on the right side (see the photo). Thread and weave the ribbons through the slits. Tape the ribbon ends to the inside front of the card. Tie and glue a bow to the top of the tree.

2. Draw a small upside-down triangle below the tree. Cut 2 slits on each side. Thread ribbon through the slits to make the tree base. Tape the ribbon to the inside front of the card. Line the inside of card with white paper to conceal the taped ribbon.

Michaels Supplies

red card stock
craft knife
assorted ribbons
white paper

RIBBON STAR

Celebrate Hanukkah with a silver Star of David.

Cut and fold the blue card stock to the desired size. Draw an equilateral triangle on the card front. Then draw an upside-down equilateral triangle, intersecting the triangles midway to form the star (see the photo). Cut slits in the card at each star corner. Thread the ribbon through the slits. Tape the ribbon to the inside front of the card. Line the inside of card with white paper to conceal the taped ribbon.

Michaels Supplies

blue card stock
craft knife
silver ribbon
white paper

WINTER WISHES

*Send snowmen and Christmas trees
to brighten a friend's day.*

Cut and fold the green card stock
to the desired size. Cut 3 (1") squares
from each handmade paper and 3
(1¼") squares from the red and white
card stock. Apply the transfers to the
handmade papers (see the photo).
Adhere the squares to each other and
to the card. Frame the card with
green handmade paper. Use the
opaque pens to draw the border.

Michaels Supplies

card stock: green, red, white
handmade papers: green, white
rub-on transfers: trees, snowmen
craft glue
opaque pens

HOW TO MAKE ENVELOPES IN 5 EASY STEPS

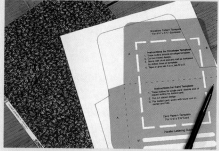

1. Trace the envelope template
onto the wrong side of the
desired paper.

2. Cut out the traced shape.
Fold and press the sides together
as indicated on the template.

3. Use the glue stick to adhere
the wrong side of the flaps to the
wrong side of envelope.

4. Glue the remaining flap to
form the back of the envelope.

5. Glue solid paper to the envelope for the mailing label.

Michaels Supplies

envelope template
paper: decorative, solid
glue stick
pen

Handmade Gifts

Warm the hearts of your loved ones with presents you've made just for them.

PILLOW PRESENT
Combine ribbon and cording to create this one-of-a-kind pillow.

1. To make the ribbon fringe, form a continuous length of 3" loops of ribbon, pinning the loops together as you work until the length measures 18". Tuck the raw ends of the ribbon inside the first and last loops. Stitch the ribbon loops together along 1 folded edge. Repeat to make another 18"-length of looped ribbon.

2. Cut a 19"-length of the ½"-wide red trim. Tuck the raw ends under and stitch the trim to the sewn folded edge of 1 looped ribbon length. Repeat with the remaining looped ribbon length.

3. Referring to the photo, place 1 looped ribbon fringe along 1 side of the pillow front, 3" from the side seam. Pin it to secure and stitch it in place. Repeat to attach the remaining looped ribbon fringe to the other side of the pillow.

4. Wrap 1 end of the cording with thread. Trim close to the wrap to prevent the cording from raveling. Beginning with the wrapped end of the cording, form "Joy" in the center of the pillow (see the photo). Pin the cording to secure it and stitch it in place. Wrap the remaining end of the cording with thread. Trim close to the wrap.

CANDY-CUP TOPIARY

Perched in a holiday coffee mug, this colorful candy tree sweetens the season.

1. Cut the craft foam block to tightly fill the inside of the cup. Press the foam inside the cup. To attach the topiary tree to the foam base, see "Topiary Base" below.

2. Following the manufacturer's instructions, use the meringue powder to make hard Royal Icing. Cover the cone and the foam inside the cup with a thick layer of icing.

3. Referring to the photo, arrange the candy sticks, candy canes, and peppermint candies on the cone and around the foam in the cup, pressing the candies firmly into the icing. Let dry. If desired, spray the candy-covered cone with acrylic sealer. Let dry. (The candy will not be edible if sprayed with the sealer.)

Michaels Supplies

craft foam block
holiday coffee cup
small craft foam cone
craft glue
assorted candy sticks, candy
    canes, and round pepper-
    mint candies
meringue powder
clear acrylic spray sealer
    (optional)

TOPIARY BASE

1. Apply glue to 1 end of 1 candy stick. Press the glue-covered end of the candy stick into the center of the foam in the cup. Apply glue to the uncovered end of the candy stick. Press the foam cone onto the candy stick.

2. We used candy sticks to decorate this topiary tree, but you can also use candy canes.

◀ BEADED STAR

Brighten a friend's day with a gift that sparkles with beads and wire.

1. Disassemble the frame. Paint the front and the sides of the frame gold. Let dry.

2. Drill a hole through the center of each star point. Thread 1" of 1 wire end from the frame front to the back through the hole in 1 star point. To secure the wire, thread 1 pony bead onto the 1" wire end, loop the wire around the bead, and pull the wire tightly through the hole to the frame front.

3. Thread 1 bead onto the wire until it meets the frame front; loop the wire close to the bead to secure. Continue adding beads and winding the wire 3 or 4 times around each star point. Do not thread beads at the frame back.

4. When all star points are covered, thread the wire end from the front through a hole to the back. Twist the end around a nearby wire on the frame back. Reassemble the frame.

Michaels Supplies

star-shaped wooden frame
metallic gold acrylic paint
paintbrush
drill with ⅛" bit
4 yards 26-gauge silver wire
wire cutters
multicolored 7-mm pony beads

Michaels Supplies

desired wooden picture frame
water-soluble pen
masking tape
desired rub-on transfers
checkerboard border stencil
small stencil brush
black acrylic paint

◀ CHECKED BORDER

Stencils and rub-ons add pizzazz to this easy-to-decorate frame.

1. Outline the frame opening on the glass, using the water-soluble pen. Disassemble the frame.

2. Place the glass on a work surface and secure it with tape. Using the outline as a guide, place the transfers above the bottom line on the glass. Following the manufacturer's instructions, apply the transfers. Remove the pen marks.

3. To create the checkered border, place the stencil as desired along the frame edge. Use the stencil brush and paint to pounce paint onto the stencil. Continue to stencil all the edges of the frame. Let dry. Reassemble the frame.

HARLEQUIN FRAME

Glittering diamonds dance around this pretty picture holder.

1. Disassemble the frame. Using a pencil and ruler, mark 2" intervals along the outer and inner edges of the frame front. Connect the marks with straight lines to form diamonds.

2. Cut the jute string into 3" to 6" lengths. Coat 1 length with wood glue. Form the string into a coil and press it onto the frame in the center of a diamond. Continue to fill the desired diamonds with jute coils. Let dry.

3. Following the manufacturer's instructions, paint the sealer over adjacent diamonds, both with and without jute coils (see the photo). Let dry. Repeat, using the base coat. Let dry. Repeat, using the adhesive. Let dry. Rub the foil onto the adhesive-covered diamonds. Paint the sealer over the foil-covered diamonds. Let dry. Finish with the tarnish antique paint.

Wipe the paint off, leaving paint only in the crevices. Let dry.

4. Paint the remaining diamonds and the edges of the frame black. Let dry. Reassemble the frame.

Michaels Supplies

desired rectangular wooden
  frame
pencil and ruler
jute string
wood glue
paintbrush
Delta Renaissance Foil Sealer
Delta Renaissance Foil
  Pewter Gray Base Coat
Delta Renaissance Foil
  Adhesive
Delta Renaissance Silver Foil
Delta Renaissance Foil Silver
  Tarnish Antique
black acrylic paint

SHINING SNOWFLAKE

Showcase a little photograph in this frame covered with sequins.

Disassemble the frame. Paint the front and the sides of the frame silver. Let dry. Pile the sequins onto the waxed paper. Spread glue over the frame front. Press the frame, glue side down, into the sequins until the frame front is covered. Gently shake off the excess sequins. Let dry. Reassemble the frame.

Michaels Supplies

snowflake-shaped wooden
  frame
metallic silver acrylic paint
paintbrush
8-mm silver cupped sequins
waxed paper
clear-drying craft glue

ANTIQUED APPLE TRAY

Transform a plain wooden tray into a custom-made accessory with stencils and paints tailored to the recipient's style.

1. Lightly sand the tray to remove rough areas on the wood. Wipe off any dust. Paint the center of the tray white. Let dry. Paint the lip of the tray dark green. Let dry. To protect the white center of the tray from additional paint, apply paint tape around the inside lip of the tray. Using the zigzag roller and light green paint, paint diagonal lines around the lip of the tray. Let dry.

2. Place a small amount of red, burgundy, orange, yellow, light green, and dark green paints onto a paper plate. Referring to the photo, paint the colors onto the apple stamp. Press the stamp onto the center of the tray. Carefully lift the stamp to remove. Let dry.

3. Referring to the photo, paint a red squiggly line around the inside edge of the tray. Let dry. Antique the tray by lightly sanding the paint away on the edges and the inside of the tray. Wipe off any dust. Apply 2 coats of clear varnish, letting dry between the coats.

Michaels Supplies

wooden tray
sandpaper
acrylic paints: white, dark
  green, light green, red,
  burgundy, orange, yellow
paintbrushes
paint tape
zigzag roller
apple stamp
clear varnish

QUICK DISH TOWELS

Create designer gifts for all your friends in no time.

For each, glue lengths of trim and buttons to each end of a dish towel (see the photo). Let dry. (If desired, stitch trim and buttons in place instead of gluing.)

Michaels Supplies

desired dish towels
assorted trims
assorted buttons
clear-drying fabric glue
    (optional)
thread to match (optional)

SHAKE IT UP

Salt-and-pepper shakers become dazzling Christmas gifts when decked with jewels and ribbon. For a different look, embellish some with rub-on transfers.

Referring to the photo, decorate each shaker as desired. Attach jewels to the shaker, using silicone sealer. Tie a bow at the top of each shaker and thread on jingle bells, if desired. Fill each shaker with a mixture of cinnamon and sugar.

Michaels Supplies

assorted glass salt-and-pepper
    shakers
glass gems in assorted colors
silicone sealer
assorted ribbons
assorted jingle bells
cinnamon and sugar

STYLISH VASES
Present winter blooms in handsome handcrafted vases.

Michaels Supplies

For the frosted vase:
clear glass vase
rubber band
1"-wide paint tape
frosted glass spray finish

For the marble vase:
small glass vase
silicone sealer
glass marbles in desired
    color (approximately 15)

To make the frosted vase, clean and dry the vase thoroughly. Mark a straight circumference line about a third of the way down the vase. Place the rubber band evenly around the mark.

Place lengths of tape vertically in ½" intervals along the top edge of the rubber band. Remove the rubber band. Following the manufacturer's instructions, spray the vase completely with the frosted glass finish. Let dry. Remove the paint tape.

To make the marble vase, clean and dry the vase thoroughly. Using the silicone sealer, randomly attach the marbles to the vase, beginning at the bottom of the vase.

SEE & DO
Frosted Vase

1. To create the design on the frosted vase, tape off stripes that will remain clear. Spray the vase with the frosted finish.

2. Let the vase dry completely before removing the paint tape.

MADONNA TRIPTYCH

Decoupage favorite Christmas cards to a wooden screen.

1. Lightly sand the screen and the blocks. Wipe off any dust. Paint the wooden blocks metallic gold. Let dry. Paint the screen blue, letting 1 side and 1 edge dry before turning over. Referring to the photo and using white paint, paint clouds on the inside panels by holding the paintbrush vertically and using only the very ends of the brush bristles. Let dry. Draw stars and dots in a random pattern on the outside panels of the screen, using the dimensional paints. Let dry.

2. Cut a picture of the Madonna from a Christmas card. Following the manufacturer's instructions, glue the cutout to the inside center panel of the screen, using the decoupage finish. Arrange stickers or the desired images on the inside side panels of the screen. Apply several coats of the decoupage finish to the inside panels of the screen. Let dry.

3. Referring to the photo, glue the gold wooden blocks to the bottom corners of the screen.

STARRY BOX

This container is just the right size to hold a season's worth of holiday cards.

1. Lightly sand the box. Wipe off any dust. Apply 1 coat of sealer to the entire box. Let dry.

2. Paint the entire box with 2 coats of purple paint, letting dry between the coats. Apply 2 coats of varnish to the entire box, letting dry between the coats.

3. Place small amounts of gold and silver paints onto separate paper plates. Dip a star sponge into the desired paint, pounce the sponge onto the plate to remove any excess paint. Sponge-paint the box. Repeat with assorted sponges to paint gold and silver stars onto the box, letting the colors overlap in some areas.

4. Paint the wooden star teal. Let dry. Referring to the photo, glue the star to the outside center of the box lid, with half of the star extending beyond the edge of the lid. Let dry.

◀ FOLK ANGEL CLOCK

The clock movement kit makes this an easy gift to assemble with style.

1. Referring to the photo, drill a hole at the top of each angel wing.

2. Paint the entire angel dark brown. Following the manufacturer's instructions, coat the edges and the front of the angel with the crackle medium. Let dry.

3. Paint the wings aqua. Paint the head and the body white. Let dry. Referring to the photo, paint the face peach. Let dry. (The crackle lines will appear as the paint begins to dry.)

4. Following the manufacturer's instructions, assemble the clock movements on the angel. Glue 1 star in each of the 12, 3, 6, and 9 o'clock positions. Let dry.

5. Cut a 36"-length of wire. Attach 1 end of the wire through the hole in 1 angel wing. Referring to the photo, loop the wire around several stars and arch it over the angel's head. Attach the remaining end of the wire through the hole in the remaining wing. Use the wire cutters to trim the extra wire.

Michaels Supplies

drill with ⅛" bit
wooden angel clock
acrylic paints: dark brown,
    aqua, white, peach
paintbrushes
crackle medium
clock movement kit
rusted tin stars
craft glue
rusted wire
wire cutters

BRIGHT BULBS ▶

Paint colorful designs onto plain wooden light bulbs for a gift to create by the dozens.

Using the desired colors of paints, paint the desired designs onto the light bulbs, letting dry between the coats.

Michaels Supplies

assorted acrylic paints
paintbrushes
wooden bulbs

FALLING SNOWFLAKES

A special friend will enjoy a gift that will keep her warm season after season.

1. Cut the ribbing away from the bottom of the sweatshirt. Serge or zigzag the raw edge to prevent raveling. Turn the bottom edge under 1¼" and stitch the hem in place.

2. Referring to the photo, pin the doilies on front of the sweatshirt. Stitch them in place. Referring to the photo and using the marker, draw loops and lines above and between the doily snowflakes; then draw 3 trees as shown along the bottom of the sweatshirt.

3. Using the chenille needle and the white floss, make large running stitches along the snowflake lines. Make large running stitches with the green floss along the tree lines.

4. Arrange the pom-poms along the bottom of the sweatshirt (see the photo). Stitch the pom-poms in place.

5. Spray the sweatshirt with a light mist of water to remove any visible marker lines.

Michaels Supplies

red sweatshirt
thread to match
assorted lace doilies
water-soluble marker
large chenille needle
embroidery floss: white, green
white pom-poms

Wrap It Up

After finding just the right gifts for everyone on your list, add to the joy with presenta~ tions that are almost too pretty to open.

Michaels Supplies

white wrapping paper
red acrylic paint
waxed paper
desired decorative sponge
    rollers and rubber stamps
ribbon and cording: red,
    white
miniature ornaments
    (optional)
berry picks (optional)

◄WRAP AND ROLL

Roller stamps let you custom-design wrapping paper and matching gift tags in mere minutes.

1. Cut the wrapping paper to the desired size for each package. Save the scraps to make gift tags.

2. Pour the paint onto the waxed paper. Referring to the photo, use the sponge rollers and the rubber stamps to apply paint as desired to the wrapping-paper pieces and to the gift tag scraps. Let dry. Wrap each box.

3. Tie the packages with ribbon or cording as desired. For each, fold a gift tag in half. Punch a hole in the top of the tag. Tie it on with ornaments or berry picks.

CHRISTMAS CART ►

Load up this subsize grocery cart with all kinds of holiday goodies, just as you would a basket.

1. Wrap a strip of wide ribbon around the center of the cart and knot it at the back. Hot-glue the back of the ribbon to the basket. Tie a multilooped bow from the same ribbon (see "Bows" on page 123) and wire it to the back of the cart.

2. Cut strips of greenery from the holly garland. Twist these strips together into a longer strand, forming arches. Hot-glue the garland to the ribbon around the basket. Hot-glue jingle bells to the garland as desired.

3. Fill the cart with bears. Tie ribbon around 1 bear's neck. Form 2 wreaths from the remaining garland strips. Place 1 wreath on top of the same bear's head. Place the other wreath around the remaining bear's neck. Hot-glue jingle bells to the wreaths as desired.

Michaels Supplies

miniature grocery cart
assorted ribbons
hot-glue gun and glue sticks
florist's wire
holly garland
small jingle bells
teddy bears (or goodies to
   fill the basket)

CYLINDER SURPRISE

The soft flocking on the tops of these containers adds to their richness. Use them to present candles and cookies.

1. Place paint tape in stripes or crisscross patterns on the papier-mâché containers. Paint each container gold between the tape and around the lip of the caps. Let dry. Remove the tape strips.

2. Lightly brush 1 layer of green paint over the entire surface of each container. Wipe off the gold areas with a paper towel. If desired, lightly touch up the gold paint.

3. Following the manufacturer's instructions, apply Soft Flock fibers to the top of each cap.

4. Fill the containers with tissue and embellish them with ribbons as desired.

Michaels Supplies

paint tape
papier-mâché containers
paintbrushes
acrylic paints: gold, green
paper towels
green Plaid Soft Flock™
desired tissue
assorted gold ribbons

PAINTED POCKETFULS

For quick holiday gifts, embellish a dozen pocketfuls and fill them with candy.

1. Referring to the photo and using a paintbrush or a sponge, paint the shapes as desired. For a suggested pattern, refer to "Easy as A-B-C" below. Let dry.

2. Use the craft tip and the paint to outline the pocketfuls in the desired colors. Let dry.

3. Glue the buttons and the beads to the pocketfuls as desired. Let dry.

Michaels Supplies

assorted wooden pocketfuls
acrylic paint in assorted
    colors
paintbrushes
paint tape (optional)
craft tip set
craft glue
assorted buttons
assorted beads

EASY AS A- B- C

A Mark a striped pattern on the pocketful with paint tape.

B Use the craft tip set and the gold paint to outline the shape.

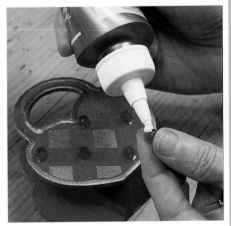

C After the paint dries, glue beads onto the pocketful.

CUTOUT GIFT BAGS

Turn corrugated craft bags into whimsical holiday sacks with the help of cookie cutters and tissue paper.

1. For each, trace the desired cookie cutter onto a paper scrap; cut out the pattern. Position the pattern on the front of the bag and lightly tape it in place. Use the craft knife to cut out the shape from the bag. For smoother edges, use repeated light strokes with the craft knife.

2. Tape cellophane and then iridescent tissue paper behind the opening. Tie a raffia bow around the handles and attach miniature ornaments to the bow.

3. To make the decorative tissue paper, use the desired stamp and the ink pad to create designs on white tissue paper. Let dry. Stuff the bag with tissue paper.

STAMPED SACKS

Embellish gift sacks and matching papier-mâché ornaments with stamped designs.

1. For each, pour acrylic paint onto waxed paper. Dip the desired rubber stamp into the paint and place on the bag where desired. Repeat as desired. Let dry.

2. Referring to the photo, paint or stamp a papier-mâché ornament as desired. Let dry.

3. Tie a bow around the handles of the sack (see "Bows" on page 123). Attach the ornament. Stuff the sack with tissue paper.

WINNING TRIMMINGS

Decorate an assortment of Christmas gift sacks with buttons, doilies, ribbons, and berries.

To make the doily sack, glue on the heart doily. For added dimension, glue a smaller circular doily in the center. Let dry. Glue the angel to the center of the second doily. Let dry. Glue a length of garland to the top of the sack. Cut individual stars from the garland. Scatter and glue them around the heart doily. Let dry. Stamp gold stars onto the tissue paper. Let dry. Stuff the sack with tissue paper.

To make the wreath sack, shape the spray into a circle. Twist the ends to hold in place. Glue it onto the sack. Glue buttons around the wreath. Glue a length of garland to the top of the sack. Let dry. Stuff the sack with cellophane.

To make the button sack, randomly glue buttons to the sack. Let dry. Glue a length of ribbon to the top of the sack. Let dry. Stuff the sack with cellophane.

Michaels Supplies

For each:
red gift sacks
hot-glue gun and glue sticks
desired tissue paper or
    cellophane
For the doily sack:
doilies: heart, smaller circle
miniature angel ornament
white star minigarland
rubber stamp
gold ink pad
For the wreath sack:
berry spray on gold wire
assorted buttons
beaded minigarland
For the button sack:
assorted buttons
desired ribbon

IN THE BAG

1. For each, lay out the desired trims before you glue them in place. That way, you can rearrange them, if desired, before they are permanently attached.

2. To fit the trim to the top edge of the sack, stretch the garland or the ribbon across the width of the sack. Then cut it to the length of the sack and glue it in place. Repeat to decorate the back, too, if desired.

STAR BRIGHT

This basket makes a great container for jars of jelly and mustard. Once the goodies are gone, the recipient can enjoy the basket for years.

Wire a multilooped bow to the basket (see "Bows" on page 123). Group the picks together as desired and wire them on top of the bow. Wrap the gifts with cellophane to make the star glow.

Michaels Supplies

florist's wire
desired ribbon
star-shaped wire basket
picks: fruit, iced rose
amber cellophane

Michaels Supplies

florist's wire
fruit-and-pine picks
hot-glue gun and glue sticks
sleigh
assorted doilies
desired ribbon
small jingle bells
amber cellophane

JINGLE-BELL SLEIGH

Deliver muffins, cookies, or fudge in this basket inspired by Santa's mode of travel.

1. Wire 2 fruit-and-pine picks together and glue them to the back of the sleigh. Referring to the photo, layer the bottom of the sleigh with doilies, letting them hang over the back and the front. Glue a length of ribbon down the center of the front doily. Tie a small bow and glue it to the front of the ribbon length. Then glue jingle bells to the ribbon length. Let dry.

2. Wrap squares of cellophane around goodies and tie them up with ribbons. Glue jingle bells to the ribbons. Let dry.

YULETIDE TULLE

Let handsome bottles shine in see-through wraps made from tulle and ribbon.

To make the plain bags (at left and right in the photo), fold a length of tulle in half. Place the bottle on the center of the tulle. Cut the folded bag 4" longer than the top of the bottle. Remove the bottle. Loosely stitch each side, leaving ½" seam; or glue the seams. Put the bottle in the bag. Tie the top with ribbon, cording, or a minigarland. Glue a miniature ornament, greenery sprig, or button to the center of the bow.

To make the ribbon-sided tulle bag (at center in the photo) for bottles that are larger than tulle could contain, glue ribbon to 1 side of the tulle. Then complete the bag as you would a plain tulle bag.

Michaels Supplies

tulle
scissors
needle and thread (optional)
hot-glue gun and glue sticks
desired ribbon and cording
star minigarland
miniature ornament (optional)
greenery sprig (optional)
desired button (optional)

TAG TOPPERS

Instead of big bows, top your packages with foam gift tags.

Place the desired cookie cutter shape on top of the foam (see the photo for colors). Cut it out with the craft knife.

To make the gingerbread man, outline the edge with red paint. Let dry. Stamp the inside with the gingerbread man stamp and white paint. Let dry.

To make the star, use smaller star cookie cutters to cut shapes from the green foam. Punch holes from the green foam. Glue the small stars and the circles to the large star.

To make the tree, outline the edge with green paint. Let dry. Stamp the tree with the small star stamp and white paint. Let dry. Cut assorted red circles and outline them with red paint. Let dry. Glue them to the tree.

To make the ornament, cut 2 strips of white foam (see the photo). Glue them to the center of the ornament. Cut a smaller circle and outline it with green paint. Let dry. Glue it to the top of the ornament. Paint red swirly lines at the bottom and the top of the ornament. Let dry.

For each, use a paint pen to write the desired name on the gift tag. Punch a hole in the top of the tag. Tie it to the package with ribbon.

Michaels Supplies

assorted cookie cutters
Fun Foam: red, white, green
craft knife
paint pens: red, green
white acrylic paint
paintbrush
rubber stamps: gingerbread
    man, small star
craft glue
hole punch
desired ribbon

Michaels Supplies

acrylic paints: black, red, white
paintbrushes
assorted oval papier-mâché
    boxes
rub-on transfers
buttons: snowmen, stars
clear acrylic spray
desired tissue paper
desired ribbon

WINTRY WRAPS

Transform papier-mâché boxes into scenes from a winter wonderland. The oval containers come in different sizes, so this idea's great to have a variety of gifts.

1. Paint the lid of each box black, the lip of each box red, and the base of each box white. Let dry.

2. Following the manufacturer's instructions, apply the rub-ons to the lids and the sides of the boxes. For added dimension, glue on snowmen and star buttons. Let dry. Spray each box with acrylic sealer. Let dry.

3. Fill the boxes with tissue paper and wrap them with ribbon.

PAPIER-MÂCHÉ EMBELLISHMENTS

1. The rub-on transfers stand out better against a black background than they would on the natural papier-mâché.

2. Paint each lid with black acrylic paint. Once it dries, it takes only a few minutes to apply the transfers.

Festive Fare

From decorations to gifts to centerpieces, these tasty treats are sure to be holiday favorites.

Michaels Supplies

2 (14-ounce) packages
    vanilla-flavored white
    candy melts
2½" cookie cutters: star,
    fruit-shaped
waxed paper
4" lollipop sticks
disposable decorating bag
decorating tip No. 3 or 4
edible white glitter (optional)
clear and decorative lollipop
    bags and twist ties
assorted ribbons
small square cardboard box
2 or 3 craft foam blocks
bubble wrap

PEARLY WHITE POPS

Plain lollipops never tasted as good as these lacy white chocolate-flavored treats.

Whip up a dazzling array of these lacy pops in a short amount of time with our simple instructions. Then place them in pretty bags to give as gifts or party favors. Or feature them in a centerpiece on your holiday table.

The lacy technique becomes easy once you pipe 1 or 2 of the pops. You can't mess up—just drizzle on more melted candy!

To melt the candy, place 1 package of candy melts in the top of a double boiler over hot—not simmering—water. Heat them until the candy melts, stirring often. Remove from the heat; let stand over hot water 5 minutes.

To make the lacy stars, trace the star cookie cutter onto several sheets of waxed paper. Turn the waxed-paper sheets over and place them on baking sheets. Put a lollipop stick at the bottom of each star so that it overlaps the star about 1".

Spoon 1 cup of melted candy into a disposable decorating bag fitted with tip No. 3 or 4. (Keep remaining melted candy warm over hot water; replenish the bag as needed.)

Referring to "Drizzle Dazzle" below, drizzle a layer of candy on the lollipops. Let them harden slightly. Then drizzle another lacy layer on each star. Sprinkle them with edible white glitter, if desired. Chill the lacy stars at least 15 minutes or until hardened. Carefully peel the hardened stars from the waxed paper. Place them in bags. Secure with twist ties and tie each with ribbon. Yield: about 3 dozen lacy stars.

To make the centerpiece package, remove the top of cardboard box. To keep the centerpiece box sturdy, place a brick or another flat, heavy object in the bottom of the box. Cut 2 or 3 blocks of foam to fit the box opening. Stack the foam on top of the brick, filling the box.

Cover the box with bubble wrap, bunching the wrap at the top. Loosely tie the bubble wrap together with a ribbon bow, leaving enough slack to insert lollipops.

Insert as many lollipops as desired into the foam box through bubble-wrap opening. Surround the centerpiece with candles, greenery, and pretty ornaments. Yield: 1 centerpiece.

COOKIE-CUTTER POPS
Wrap in Della Robbia treat bags.

Melt 1 package of candy in the top of the double boiler(see "To melt the candy" at left). Draw an 8" x 9" rectangle on a sheet of waxed paper. Turn the paper over and place it on a baking sheet. Spread the melted candy evenly, about ¼" thick, to fill out the dimensions of the rectangle. Let stand at room temperature 35 minutes until almost firm.

Cut out pineapples, apples, and other designs, using a cookie cutter. Apply gentle pressure with your fingers to penetrate the candy and to help remove candy from the tips of each cutter. (Dip a cookie cutter in hot water first and then wipe it dry. Press the warm cutter immediately into the almost-firm candy. Release the candy from the cutter very carefully.)

Attach lollipop sticks to the back of each pop, using the remaining melted candy as glue. Let them harden. Place them in lollipop bags as directed for the lacy stars. Yield: about 1½ dozen solid pops, depending on the shapes used.

DRIZZLE DAZZLE
Lacy Stars

1. Outline each star with melted candy.

2. Drizzle the melted candy in a lacy design to fill each star, covering the lollipop stick thoroughly.

GINGERBREAD VILLAGE PHOTO FRAMES

A ready-made village comes to life when you decorate it with photos of adorable little ones. No baking is required!

A ready-to-decorate Gingerbread Village Kit is easy and fun for the whole family to make. It's even more special when you turn the building fronts into holiday photo frames of your children. Four colors of icing and a good assortment of colorful candies are included in the kit, along with the prebaked gingerbread.

If you can't bare to spare favorite photos, use a computer scanner or a color copy machine to reproduce duplicates at minimal cost. To protect the originals or the copies from moisture, spray the photos with clear glaze and let them dry overnight before attaching to them the gingerbread.

To begin, select a gingerbread village building front. Trim the desired photos to fit in the frames.

Prepare the colored icings. Place them in separate decorating bags, according to the package directions. (Icing dries out quickly, so keep the bag covered with a damp cloth.)

"Glue" each photo to a frame with white icing (see "See & Do," Step 1). Pipe the icing around picture (see Step 2) and place candies on the piped icing if desired. Let dry at least 3 hours.

Pipe or spread a generous amount of the icing on the back of the frame where the gingerbread easel will go. Press the easel into the icing (see Step 3). Let dry at least 3 hours with the easel side up. Repeat for the remaining frames.

Stand the frames upright on a cardboard base. Pave a walkway with additional frosting. Sprinkle coconut "snow" to cover the cardboard.

Stored in a cool, dry place, the photo frames should last for several years.

SEE & DO

1. Pipe a small amount of icing at each corner on the back of a photo. Press the photo where desired on the gingerbread.

2. Pipe around the photo with the desired color of icing to secure it. Decorate the front of the frame. Let it dry thoroughly.

3. Pipe icing on the back of the frame as shown. Press the easel into the icing to enable the frame to stand.

Michaels Supplies

1 (3.25-pound) Wilton's
    Gingerbread Village Kit
desired photos
glaze spray
cardboard or plywood base
grated coconut

CHRISTMAS CRANBERRY SALAD ▶

The fruit relief on this mold shows up beautifully, so give the salad a prime location on the buffet table.

Shape this crimson-colored salad in our new Della Robbia-inspired mold to make a salad that's pretty enough to be the centerpiece.

Cranberry Salad

1 envelope unflavored gelatin
¼ cup cold water
2 (3-ounce) packages lemon-flavored gelatin
3 cups boiling water
3 tablespoons grated orange rind
⅓ cup fresh orange juice
4 cups fresh cranberries
2 cups sugar
1 cup mayonnaise
1 (8-ounce) carton sour cream
Garnishes: fresh cranberries, fresh mint sprigs

Sprinkle the gelatin over the cold water in a large bowl; stir and let it stand 1 minute. Add the lemon flavored gelatin and the boiling water; stir 2 minutes or until the gelatin dissolves. Chill until it achieves the consistency of an unbeaten egg white, about 30 minutes.

Position a knife blade in food the processor bowl. Add the orange rind, juice, and cranberries; process 1 minute. Combine the cranberry mixture and the sugar in a bowl; let it stand 15 minutes or until the sugar dissolves.

Stir the cranberry mixture into the gelatin mixture. Pour it into a lightly oiled Della Robbia mold. Cover and chill it until firm. Unmold it onto a serving plate.

Combine the mayonnaise and the sour cream, stirring until blended. Spoon into center of gelatin ring. Garnish, if desired. Yield: 12 servings.

Michaels Supplies

ingredients for Cranberry Salad
Della Robbia pan
food processor
large flat-bottomed serving plate

Michaels Supplies

ingredients for Butter Cookies
Santa's Treats Stamp-n-Color Cookie Making Kit
meringue powder
paste food coloring: red or green
24" length ⅜"-wide satin ribbon for each ornament
2 ring-shaped candies for each ornament

1. Press each ball of dough gently with the desired cookie stamp to flatten it and to imprint the design.

2. Dip the brush into the desired color of paint. Gently brush the paint evenly onto the cookie.

3. Fold the ribbon in half lengthwise. Place the folded end into the icing; then top with a second cookie.

4. Thread 2 candies onto the ribbon. Push the candies flush against the joined cookies.

DELICIOUS DECORATIONS

Homemade cookie ornaments are all the rage, especially when you personalize them with a Stamp-n-Color cookie kit.

To give these shortbread cookies whimsical holiday shapes and colors, imprint them with our decorative stamps and then paint them with the festive food colors. Once the cookies are baked and painted, go ahead and indulge your temptation to devour a few. They're very rich and buttery. But hold back an assortment to hang on the Christmas tree.

Butter Cookies

1 cup butter, softened
1 cup sugar
1 large egg
1 teaspoon vanilla extract
3 cups all-purpose flour
Vegetable cooking spray
Additional all-purpose flour

To make the cookies, beat the butter at medium speed of an electric mixer until creamy; gradually add the sugar, beating well. Add the egg, beating just until blended; stir in the vanilla. Gradually add the flour, beating well. (The dough will be firm.)

Roll the dough into 1½" balls and place them on an ungreased cookie sheet. Lightly spray the cookie stamps with cooking spray. Dip them into additional flour and shake off the excess flour. Press each dough ball down with the desired stamp (see "Step by Step," Step 1). Lift and release the stamp carefully. Bake the cookies at 350° for 12 to 15 minutes or until the edges are lightly browned. Remove the cookies from the pan. Place them on a wire rack. Let them cool.

Pour each color of paint into a small bowl. Use the brush to paint the cookies (see Step 2). Let dry overnight (paint does not harden completely). Yield: about 2½ dozen cookies (15 ornaments).

To assemble the ornaments, prepare 1 cup Royal Icing, using the meringue powder and following the manufacturer's instructions. Color the icing, if desired, using a small amount of paste food coloring for each color. Keep the icing covered with a damp paper towel, as the icing dries out quickly.

Spread a small amount (about 1½ tablespoons) of Royal Icing on the back of 1 cookie. Add a ribbon loop to 1 cookie (see Step 3). Quickly place a second cookie over the ribbon and the icing, pressing gently to sandwich the cookies together.

Thread 2 ring-shaped candies onto each cookie (see Step 4). Let the icing dry thoroughly overnight before hanging the ornaments. Use the free ends of the ribbon to tie the ornaments onto tree branches.

Christmas Is for Kids

Let your kids' creativity shine with these easy~ to~make gifts and party favors.

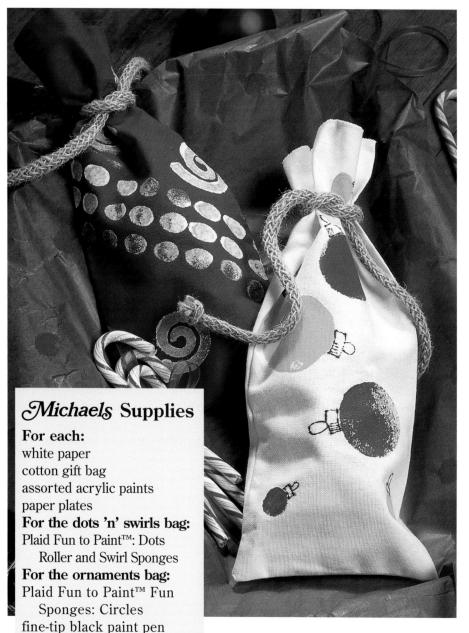

TREAT BAGS

Jazz up plain canvas gift bags for the holidays with stamps and acrylic paints.

To make the dots 'n' swirls bag, fold the sheet of paper in half and place it inside the gift bag to prevent the paint from bleeding. Squeeze white paint onto the paper plate. Roll the dotted roller through the paint and then roll it across gift bag. Dip the swirl sponge into the white paint and stamp it several times on each side of the dots. Let dry. Repeat on the opposite side of the bag.

To make the Christmas ornaments bag, fold the sheet of paper in half and place it inside the gift bag to prevent the paint from bleeding. Squeeze the paints in puddles onto paper plates. Dip the circle stamp into the desired color of paint. Stamp on 1 side of the bag. Repeat with the remaining size stamps, cleaning the stamps between each color. Let dry. Repeat on the other side of the bag. Using the black paint pen, draw a cap and hanger on each circle.

BEADED CRITTERS

Children will enjoy crafting these creatures to attach to their backpacks and purses.

Follow manufacturer's instructions to complete each animal.

Michaels Supplies

The Original Beady Buddy's™ Bead Kit: Furry Buddy's (Kit includes beads, cord, and key ring.)

PICK A KIT

There is a wide variety of kits available that let kids create all kinds of animals. The best part is that everything needed to put together bead buddies is in one kit.

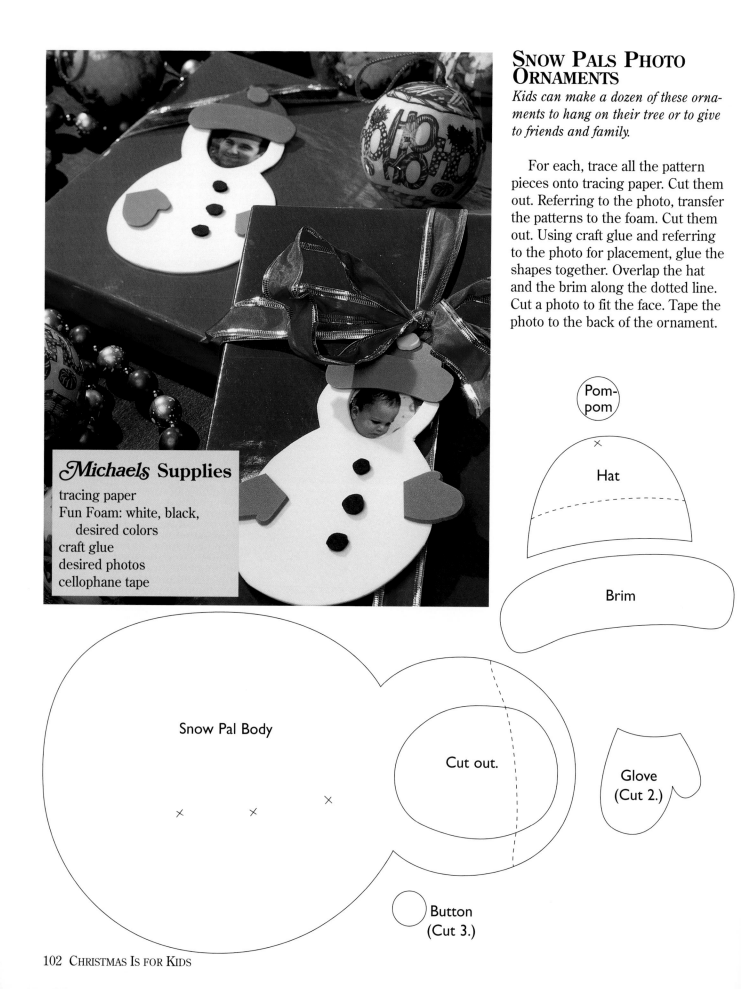

SNOW PALS PHOTO ORNAMENTS

Kids can make a dozen of these ornaments to hang on their tree or to give to friends and family.

For each, trace all the pattern pieces onto tracing paper. Cut them out. Referring to the photo, transfer the patterns to the foam. Cut them out. Using craft glue and referring to the photo for placement, glue the shapes together. Overlap the hat and the brim along the dotted line. Cut a photo to fit the face. Tape the photo to the back of the ornament.

Michaels **Supplies**

tracing paper
Fun Foam: white, black,
    desired colors
craft glue
desired photos
cellophane tape

Pom-pom

Hat

Brim

Snow Pal Body

Cut out.

Glove
(Cut 2.)

Button
(Cut 3.)

MERRY MAGNETS

Use these personalized magnets to keep everyone's wish list in place.

1. Following the manufacturer's instructions, mix the needed amount of plaster. Pour the plaster into the desired molds.

2. Let the plaster set in the molds for approximately 1 hour. After the plaster has set, gently pop the pieces from the molds. To quick-dry the plaster in the microwave, place the pieces onto paper towels in the microwave. Microwave them on LOW or DEFROST for 3 minutes. Cool 1 minute. (Do not skip the cooling time.) Microwave 3 minutes. Cool 1 minute. Microwave 3 minutes. Then let them cool to touch. To air-dry, let the plaster set in the molds for approximately 24 to 36 hours, depending on the humidity.

3. Paint the pieces as desired. Let dry. Coat them with gloss glaze. Let dry. Hot-glue a magnet to the back of each plaster piece. Let dry.

Michaels Supplies

Faster Plaster™
Faster Plaster Mold:
    Patchwork Pals (or
    Christmas mold of your
    choice)
Faster Plaster paints
fine-point paintbrushes
Faster Plaster Gloss Glaze
hot-glue gun and glue sticks
round magnets

FASTER PLASTER FUN

1. The Faster Plaster molds make it easy to shape the magnets. Simply mix the plaster and pour it into the desired molds.

2. Paint your Faster Plaster creations with a fine-point paintbrush and Faster Plaster paints. The grooves that the molds leave on the plaster shapes make them easy to paint.

Ornaments Galore

Ornaments are perhaps the most magical element of the season.
Craft some of these charming ones to add to your collection.

SPECTACULAR SPARKLE

Your tree is sure to shine with these ornaments made of silver and gold.

To make the glitter ball, remove the cap from the ball and put the nozzle of the acrylic spray sealer up to the opening. Carefully spray the inside of the ball, rotating the ball as you spray to coat entirely. Working quickly, insert a funnel into the opening and pour in glitter. Remove the funnel and rotate the ball to cover the inside with glitter. Repeat as necessary to cover any blank spots. When satisfied with the results, turn the ball upside down and shake out any excess glitter. Replace the cap. Tie ribbon in a bow and hot-glue it to the top of the ball. Let dry. (You may also use clear or colored beads or small sequins to decorate the inside of a glass ball.)

To make the silver swirl ball, use the dimensional paint to embellish the glass ball with swirl designs as desired. Let dry. Tie ribbon in a bow and hot-glue it to the top of the ball. Let dry.

To make the shining star, decorate a papier-mâché star with ribbon and paint. Paint the front and the back of the star white, letting 1 side dry before turning it over. Cut ribbons slightly longer than needed for the desired design. On the front of the star, glue the ribbons in place, folding and gluing the ends to the sides. Let dry. Repeat on the remaining side to continue the design. Glue the desired ribbon to the side of the star, covering the ends; overlap the ends of the ribbon slightly and trim the excess. Let dry. Tie a length of ribbon in a bow. Hot-glue it to the top of the star. Let dry.

SHELL-COVERED BALL

The different colors and shapes of the shells make for an interesting ornament.

1. To make this ornament, first brush craft glue on a small area of the foam ball. Lightly press shells onto the glue-covered area. Repeat to cover the ball with shells, letting each area dry slightly before adding glue and shells to the next area. Let dry.

2. Holding several lengths as one, tie raffia in a bow, leaving a loop for a hanger. Hot-glue it to the top of the ball. Let dry.

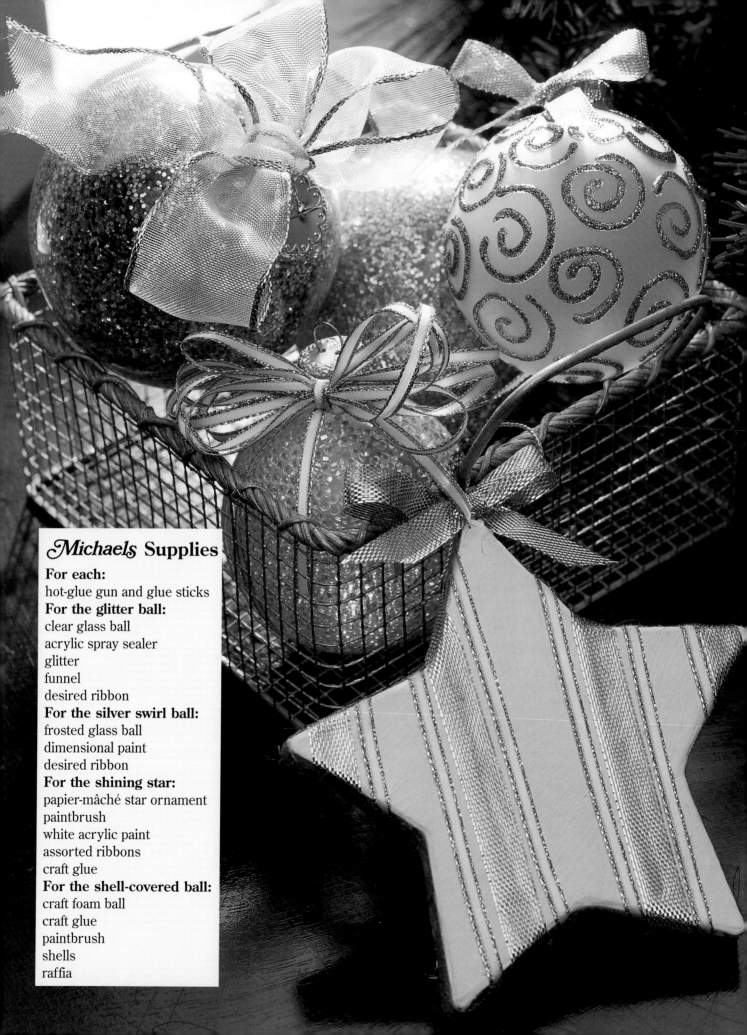

Michaels Supplies

For each:
hot-glue gun and glue sticks
For the glitter ball:
clear glass ball
acrylic spray sealer
glitter
funnel
desired ribbon
For the silver swirl ball:
frosted glass ball
dimensional paint
desired ribbon
For the shining star:
papier-mâché star ornament
paintbrush
white acrylic paint
assorted ribbons
craft glue
For the shell-covered ball:
craft foam ball
craft glue
paintbrush
shells
raffia

Michaels Supplies

For the ribbon-wrapped ball:
craft glue
craft foam ball
assorted ribbons
straight pins
hot-glue gun and glue sticks
jingle bells

For the beaded ball:
paintbrush
craft glue
craft foam ball
beads
desired ribbon
hot-glue gun and glue sticks

For the jewel-zone ball:
E-6000
acrylic jewels
frosted glass ball
dimensional paint
desired ribbon
hot-glue gun and glue sticks

For the cording-covered ball:
desired cording
cellophane tape
paintbrush
craft glue
craft foam ball
straight pins
tassel
hot-glue gun and glue sticks
desired ribbon

For the beaded Santa kit:
Sulyn brand ornament kit

SPOTLIGHT ON RED

Highlight the color of the season with trims, such as ribbon, cording, and beads.

To make the ribbon-wrapped ball, dot craft glue on the bottom of the ball. Press 1 end of the ribbon into the glue; pin it in place. Wrap the ribbon to the top of the ball and pin it in place. Repeat wrapping and pinning to cover the ball, overlapping the edges of the ribbon and covering the heads of the pins (see the photo). When the ball is completely covered, trim the excess ribbon. Glue and then pin the cut end in place. Let dry. Tie the desired ribbon in a multilooped bow, leaving a hanger. Hot-glue it to the top of the ball. Let dry. Tie 1 jingle bell to the end of each ribbon tail. Then tie 1 small bow at the top of each jingle bell.

To make the beaded ball, brush 1 small area of the foam ball with craft glue. Sprinkle beads onto the glue-covered area; lightly press them in place. Repeat to cover the ball, letting each area dry slightly before continuing. Let dry completely. Cut a length of ribbon. Fold it in half and hot-glue the ends to the ball. Holding 1 length of each color as one, tie 2 coordinating ribbons in a bow. Then hot-glue the bow in place to cover the ends of the ribbon hanger. Let dry.

To make the jewel-zone ball, glue acrylic jewels to the ball, using E-6000. Let dry. Outline each jewel with dimensional paint. Let dry. Tie a ribbon in a multilooped bow and hot-glue it to the top of the ball. Let dry

To make the cording-covered ball, prevent raveling by wrapping each end of the cord with cellophane tape. Brush 1 coat of craft glue on a small area at the bottom of ball. Press 1 end of cording into the glue and pin it in place. Wrap the cording, pressing it into the glue and securing it with pins at intervals. Apply more glue as needed and continue wrapping to cover the ball (see "See & Do" below). Let dry; then remove the pins. Wrap the tassel loop around the top of the tassel and hot-glue the loop in place. Let dry. Hot-glue the top of the tassel to the bottom of the ball. Let dry. Cut and fold a length of ribbon in half. Hot-glue the ends to the top of the ball. Let dry. Then make a multilooped bow and hot-glue in it place to cover the ends of the ribbon. Let dry.

To make the beaded Santa kit, we've done the shopping for you—just grab a Sulyn ornament kit (available in a variety of styles) that includes everything you need.
   Following the manufacturer's instructions, embellish the forms that come in the kit with beads, sequins, and trims.

SEE & DO
Cording Covered

1. Apply glue to a small area of the ball as you wrap the cording around it. To keep the cording in place, periodically pin it to the ball.

2. Pull the cording tightly as you wrap and completely cover the ball. Once the glue dries, remove the pins.

Fab Photo Frames

Let family and friends hang out on the tree in decorative papier-mâché frames.

To make the square frame, paint the front and the back of the square, letting 1 side dry before turning it over. (Be sure to keep paint out of the opening for the photo.) Glue the snowflakes to the front of the frame as desired. Let dry. Tie the ribbon in a bow and hot-glue to the top of the frame (see photo). Let dry. Insert the photo.

To make the tree frame, paint the front and the back of the tree, letting 1 side dry before turning it over. (Be sure to keep paint out of the opening for the photo.) Let dry. Glue the glass star to the top of the tree. Then glue beads to the tree as desired. Let dry. Insert the photo.

To make the diamond frame, paint the front and the back of the diamond, letting 1 side dry before turning it over. Then paint the sides. (Be sure to keep paint out of the opening for the photo.) Let dry. Cut a length of cord to fit inside the photo frame. Glue it in place. Let dry. Following the manufacturer's instructions, embellish with the rub-ons as desired. Insert the photo.

Michaels Supplies

For each:
desired papier-mâché ornament
paintbrush
acrylic paints in desired colors
low-temp glue gun and glue
    sticks
desired photo
For the square frame:
1" white iridescent sequin
    snowflakes
craft glue
desired ribbon
For the tree frame:
1 glass star
beads: gold, assorted
For the diamond frame:
2-mm red satin cord
craft glue
desired rub-on transfers

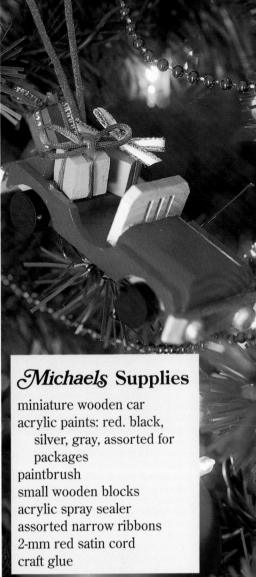

SEASONAL SHAPES

Small ornaments can liven up packages, in addition to the tree.

Note: For each ornament, follow the manufacturer's instructions to make the form.

To make the gingerbread man, letting dry between colors, on the front of the ornament, paint the body brown and the vest red; fill in the holes in the face with white, using a toothpick. Paint the back of the gingerbread man brown; let dry. Letting 1 side dry before turning over, apply 1 coat of sealer to the front and the back. Let dry. Tie ribbon in a bow. Referring to the photo, glue it in place. Let dry. Fold a length of ribbon in half. Hot-glue the ends to the back for a hanger. Let dry.

To make the holly, letting dry between colors, on the front of the ornament, paint the leaves green and the berries red. Let dry. Repeat to paint the back. Letting 1 side dry before turning over, apply 1 coat of sealer to the front and the back. Let dry. Fold ribbon in half and hot-glue the ends to the back for a hanger. Let dry.

To make the wreath, letting dry between colors, on the front of the ornament, paint the greenery green, the stars yellow, and the bow red. Let dry. Paint the back green; let dry. Letting 1 side dry before turning it over, apply 1 coat of sealer to the front and the back. Let dry. Fold the ribbon in half and hot-glue the ends to the back for a hanger. Let dry.

SPECIAL DELIVERY

Celebrate the childlike magic of the holidays with an embellished automobile.

Letting dry between colors, paint the automobile body red, the wheels black, the bumpers silver, and the windshield gray. Then paint the blocks as desired. Let dry. Spray the automobile and the blocks with acrylic sealer. Let dry. For each present, wrap a ribbon around a wooden block and tie it in a bow at the top. Glue the packages in the back of the automobile, stacking and offsetting them as desired. Fold a length of satin cord in half. Glue the ends to back of the automobile for a hanger. Let dry.

Christmas Candlelight

Add a warm glow to the holiday season with these ideas for embellishing and making candles.

Michaels Supplies
assorted ivory pillar candles
hot-glue gun and glue sticks
glass gems in desired colors
clear glass candle plate

Note: Never leave lit candles unattended.

◀ BEJEWELED BEAUTIES
Romance is in the air as soft candlelight is reflected in the glass baubles adorning these candles.

For each candle, glue gems as desired around the pillar. For a polished look, glue additional gems around the rim of the glass candle plate. Then arrange the candles on the plate.

HOLIDAY CANDLEHOLDERS ▶
Made from permanent materials, these candleholders can be used year after year.

1. To make each base for a conventional candlestick, push a nail through the small end of a cork that fits into the candlestick. Insert the nail into the bottom of a foam ball. Insert a plastic taper candleholder into the top of the foam ball (opposite the cork).
2. Cover the foam ball and the cork with sheet moss, using glue or florist's pins. Referring to the photo, glue or pin ribbon, holly leaves, and berries to the ball. Place the ball in the candlestick and insert a candle into the plastic candleholder.

Michaels Supplies

2" x 2" nails
corks
craft foam balls
plastic taper candleholders
sheet moss
hot-glue gun and glue sticks
    or florist's pins
assorted ribbons
holly leaves
berries
candlesticks
taper candles

Michaels Supplies

craft knife
ruler
beeswax sheets: ivory, honey
candle wicking
star cookie cutters or stencils

STARS AND STRIPES

Use beeswax sheets for a fast and inexpensive way to create your own designer candles.

To make the striped candle, using a craft knife and a ruler, cut 3 (1" x 16") lengths of each color of beeswax. Place the strips side by side on a flat surface, alternating the colors and overlapping the long edges approximately ¼". Gently press the overlapped edges so that they stick together.

Place a 7" length of wicking across 1 short edge of the layered wax strips. Beginning at the wick end, roll the candle firmly. (The firmer you roll the candle, the longer it will burn.) At room temperature, the wax is pliable and slightly sticky, so it can be molded and shaped as it is rolled.

To make the 8" star pillar, use a craft knife to cut an 8" x 16" piece of ivory wax. **To make the 4" star pillar,** cut a 4" x 16" piece of ivory wax. **For each,** cut a length of wicking 1" longer than the height of the candle. Place the length of wicking across 1 short edge of the piece of wax. Working on a flat surface and beginning at the wick end, roll the candle firmly (see "See & Do" at left).

Using the cookie cutters or the stencils, cut out a variety of star shapes from the honey-colored beeswax. Gently press the star shapes onto the rolled candle as desired. (At room temperature the wax is pliable and slightly sticky, so the stars should adhere.)

SEE & DO
Beeswax Candles

1. Cut a length of wicking that is slightly longer than the height of the candle. Roll the edge of the beeswax over the wick, keeping the wick taut and pressing the beeswax against the wick to secure.

2. Continue rolling evenly and fairly tightly toward the opposite end. Press the outside edge of the beeswax against the candle to seal.

CHRISTMAS CONFETTI

Bejeweled and bedecked candles and accessories transform your home into a celebration of the season.

To make the jeweled candles and candleholders, glue glass gems as desired to votive candles, pillar candles, clear glass votive holders, and clear glass plates with craft glue. For a creative twist, turn some candleholders upside down and set the candle on top of them rather than in them.

To make the dimensional tapers and candleholders, apply dots, in alternating colors of dimensional paints, around the taper or the candleholder. Also use dimensional paints on votive candles. To embellish a votive candle like the red one in the center of the photo above, use the tip of the paints like a pen to add swirls, stars, and holly leaves.

To make the gilded striped pillar, tape stripes down the sides of a pillar candle. Using your fingers, rub silver gilding paint over the uncovered areas of the candle. Let dry. Remove the tape.

To make the beaded votive holders, wrap a length of wire around a votive candleholder to determine the amount you will need. To secure the first bead, insert 1 end of the wire through the hole in 1 bead, pull the wire up the side of the bead, insert the wire in the hole again, and then fold the short end of the wire into the hole. For added security, apply a small amount of glue into the bead hole. String a variety of beads onto the length of wire. Secure the last bead as you did the first. Wrap the beaded wire around the sides of the votive candleholder. Use dots of hot glue to hold the beaded wire in place on the candleholder. Create additional beaded wire lengths to use as garlands to weave throughout your arrangement.

Michaels Supplies

assorted candles: red tapers, white pillars, red and white votives
assorted glass candleholders: votive, taper
glass candle plate
assorted acrylic jewels
E-6000
dimensional paints: red, green, silver, and gold
masking tape
silver gilding paint
florist's wire
assorted beads
hot-glue gun and glue sticks

POURED PERFECTION

Create candles in shapes as unique
as your decorating style.

1. Referring to the manufacturer's instructions, prepare the candle mold. Put layers of wax chunks, adding botanicals if desired, into the mold, filling to within 1" of the top. (Whatever is placed in the candle mold first will be at the top of the finished candle; conversely, whatever is placed last will be at the bottom.) Insert the wick. Tie it to the skewer to hold it in place.

2. Break the clear wax block into chunks small enough to fit into the melting pitcher. Melt the wax on the stove on medium-high heat. Continue to add wax pieces until you have filled at least half of the pitcher. Insert the thermometer into the melted wax. When the temperature reaches 200°, refer to the manufacturer's directions and put in 1 tablespoon of E-Z wax release per pound of wax, plus 1 tablespoon of translucent crystals. For a scented candle, also add an eighth of the block of candle scent.

3. Slowly pour the melted wax into the mold, tilting the mold slightly. (Reserve at least 1 cup of wax to add to the mold once the candle has settled.) Let the candle sit for 45 minutes. Use a wooden skewer to poke 2 or 3 holes near the wick. Heat the reserved wax to 190° and fill the well that has formed on the candle from settling. Let the candle sit for 45 minutes. Repeat at least 2 more times. Let the candle sit overnight.

4. Unscrew the screw at the base of the candle mold. Use the wooden skewer to pull the pillar from the mold. Trim the wick-tied skewer from the pillar and turn the pillar right side up.

Michaels Supplies

desired metal candle molds
wax chunks: red, yellow, green
dried botanicals (optional)
clear candle wax block
metal melting pitcher with spout
candle thermometer
E-Z wax release
translucent crystals
candle scent (optional)
2 wooden skewers

MOLDING MAGIC
Chunky Candles

1. Use a screwdriver or an ice pick to break the clear wax block into pieces small enough to fit into the melting pitcher.

2. Fill the pitcher with layers of wax chunks. Tie the wick to the skewer to hold it in place.

TERRA-COTTA TREASURES ▶

Make enchanting luminaries in three easy steps.

1. Use the gold paint pen to draw dots or swirls on the pots. Let dry. Use the silver paint pen to add dots on the gold background.

2. Cover the bottom of the hole in each pot with tape. Fill the large pots with wax crystals and insert candlewicks. Place a votive candle into each small pot.

3. To finish, tie a length of ribbon around the rim of each pot.

GIFT-WRAP CANDLE

An overlay of gorgeous wrapping paper elevates a common candle to a pillar with panache.

1. Cut a piece of gift wrap wide enough to wrap around the candle with an 1" overlap. Brush a coat of glue on the back of the paper. Wrap the paper around the candle and smooth, cut any wrinkles. Then apply another coat of glue to the front of the paper. Let dry.

2. Break the wax into chunks small enough to fit into the melting pitcher. Melt the wax on the stove on medium-high heat. Continue to add wax pieces until the level of the melted wax is equal to the height of the candle. Insert the thermometer into the melted wax. When the temperature reaches 200°, refer to the manufacturer's directions and add the translucent crystals.

3. Holding the covered candle by the wick, slowly lower it into the melted wax. Carefully remove the candle from the wax. Let it cool slightly. Repeat this process 2 or 3 more times, letting the candle cool slightly between dippings. Let the candle set for 24 hours.

4. Tie a bow around the candle. Place it on a candle plate.

Michaels Supplies

paint pens: gold, silver
assorted terra-cotta pots
cellophane tape
white wax crystals
wax-coated candlewicks
white votive candles
assorted ribbons

Michaels Supplies

gift wrap
pillar candle
sponge paintbrush
craft glue
clear candle-wax block
metal melting pitcher with
    spout
candle thermometer
translucent crystals
desired ribbon
fluted clear glass candle plate

Personal & Memorable

*Start and record Christmas traditions
with some of these jovial ideas.*

BIRDHOUSE ASSEMBLY

Create a Christmas village that's personalized by each family member.

Michaels Supplies

sandpaper
assorted wooden birdhouses
assorted colors of acrylic
    paints
paintbrushes
sponges
balsa wood
craft knife
assorted wooden shapes
craft glue

To make each birdhouse, lightly sand the birdhouse. Wipe off any dust with a cloth. Prime the birdhouse with white paint. Once the birdhouse is decorated, paint a balsa sign and glue it to the birdhouse as desired.

To make Sunflower Shack, sponge-paint the house blue, the base green, and the roof silver and gray. Referring to the photo, paint wooden flowers. Cut leaves from balsa and paint them. Glue pieces to the birdhouse as desired.

To make Watermelon Stand, sponge-paint the house red and black and the roof green. Paint the wooden watermelons and the watering can. Glue them to the birdhouse.

To make Boyd's Farm, paint the birdhouse red and the base green. Sponge-paint the roof black. Let dry. Paint popsicle sticks white. Glue them to the birdhouse. Paint the wooden cows and chickens. Glue them to the birdhouse.

To make Scott's Landing, paint the birdhouse red and the roof gray. Let dry. Sponge-paint the house brown and the roof silver. Paint the wooden paddle and pail as desired. Glue them to birdhouse as desired.

To make Betsy's Art Shop, paint the entire birdhouse house yellow. Let dry. Sponge-paint the house green, the roof blue, and the pedestal brown. Make a ladder from balsa wood. Paint the ladder red. Glue it to the treehouse.

To make Margaret's Interiors, sponge-paint the birdhouse yellow and the roof blue. Glue the fence to the birdhouse. Wire the flowers to the fence.

To make Robin's Nest, sponge-paint the birdhouse gray and the roof copper. Glue the fence to the birdhouse. Paint the smaller birdhouse and birds as desired. Glue them to the big birdhouse.

To make Our Church, paint the roof brown. Let dry. Sponge-paint the roof copper. Cut windows and a cross from balsa. Paint the windows and the cross. Glue to the birdhouse.

EMBELLISHED BALSA
Our Church

1. Create shapes from balsa and glue them to the birdhouses to add character.

2. The balsa windows on this birdhouse are painted different colors and outlined in black.

PURCHASED WOODEN SHAPES
Scott's Landing

1. The paddle and the pail are purchased wooden shapes. Paint the shapes. Then glue them to the birdhouse as desired.

2. The signs on this and the other birdhouses are made from balsa.

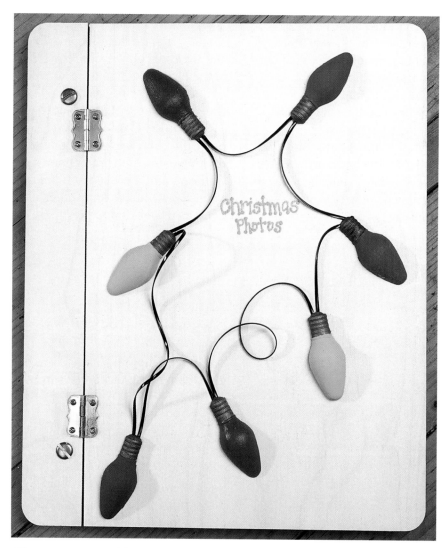

1. Use the sponge brush to lightly apply stain to the wooden album.

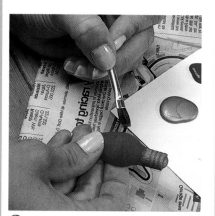

2. Once the gold paint on the bulb dries, apply paint to the rest of the bulb with a small paintbrush.

3. Apply a small amount of glue to the bulb and the cord. Tuck the cord underneath the bulb. Hold them in place.

CHRISTMAS-LIGHTS ALBUM

White-wash a plain wooden album and decorate it with a colorful display of Christmas lights.

1. Remove the cap screws to separate the album front cover from the back cover.

2. Paint the white stain on the front and back covers of the album. Let dry. Paint the bases of the wooden light bulbs gold. Let dry. Paint the rest of the light bulbs in the desired colors. Let dry.

3. Glue the bulbs to the album, tucking strands of cording under each bulb (see the photos). Use the gold opaque pen to write as desired on the center of the album.

Michaels Supplies

wooden album
White Lightning white stain and sealer
paintbrushes: flat, sponge
acrylic paints: gold, red, yellow, purple, green
split Christmas light bulb wooden shapes (flat on 1 side)
craft glue
black cording
gold opaque marker

ELEGANT PRESENTATION

This gift-wrapped album makes a handsome storage for Christmas photos and other mementos.

1. Remove the cap screws to separate the album front cover from the back cover. Cut 4 pieces of wrapping paper slightly larger than the covers. Use the spray adhesive to mount the paper to the inside of the back cover. Trim any excess paper with the craft knife. Repeat to adhere paper to the inside of the front cover and the outside back cover. Trim slits around the hinges on the front inside cover.

2. Before applying the paper to the front cover, use masking tape to cover the hinges. Spray-mount the paper to the album front. Trim paper from the outer edges, through the hinge slit, and around the hinges.

3. Hot-glue the corded trim to the outer edges of the back cover. Hot-glue the desired trim to the front cover, easing the cording in the hinge area to allow the cover to be opened. Remove the masking tape from each hinge. Glue gold trim around each hinge.

4. Make a 2½"-diameter circle on the posterboard. Write the album title as desired with the black marker. Use spray adhesive to glue the label to the front cover. Outline the label with the desired trim. Reassemble the album.

Michaels Supplies

wooden photo album
desired wrapping paper
spray adhesive
craft knife
masking tape
hot-glue gun and glue sticks
trims: cording, braid, small
   gold
compass
small posterboard
black marker

FAMILY CELEBRATION

Use these photo pages as guides to showcase your holiday gatherings.

1. Write the heading on a diamond of white paper. Outline the diamond with stitch marks, using the acid-free pen.

2. Cut 2 equal-size squares each from red and red plaid papers. Cut each square in quarters diagonally. (There should be 8 right triangles of each color.) Referring to the photo pages, arrange and tape these on the diamonds.

3. Cut 1 equal-size square of each from red, red plaid, red heart, green gingham, and green plaid papers. Fill in the remaining white space on the album page with these triangles.

4. Arrange the photos on the pages in a checkerboard pattern, with square photos in each corner and in the center of each page. Use diamond-shaped photos in the spaces around the center photo.

5. Cut 16 small strips of white paper. Write captions using the pen. Mount the captions above or below the photos.

Michaels Supplies

12" x 12" acid-free papers:
  white, red
black acid-free pen
Paperbilities III decorative
  papers
album pages
desired photos
acid-free adhesives

CANDY-CANE CHRISTMAS

Highlight photos with festive frames.

Cover the album page with the green ribbon decorative paper. Crop the photos as desired. Cut candy canes from the decorative paper and border the photos with them. Use the peel-and-stick green letters and numbers to create a heading for the page.

Michaels Supplies

album page
desired photos
decorative papers: green ribbon, Christmas candy cane
Creative Letters peel-and-stick green letters and numbers
acid-free adhesives

COOKIE SWAP

The cookies decorative paper makes a festive embellishment for this page.

1. Cover the page with red paper. Crop the photos as desired. Mat each photo on green paper.

2. Cut 3 rectangles from the white paper. Draw a red border around the edge of the rectangles. Write the heading in 1 rectangle, the story in another, and the cookie recipe in the remaining rectangle.

3. Cut cookie shapes from the cookies decorative paper and glue them to the page as desired.

Michaels Supplies

12" x 12" acid-free papers: red, green, white
Quick and Easy Christmas cookies decorative paper
assorted acid-free markers
acid-free adhesives

Christmas Basics

*Make use of this essential information
to create great~looking holiday decorations.*

CHRISTMAS TOOL KIT

It's easy to decorate your home for the holidays when you have everything that you need at your fingertips. The following is a must-have list for seasonal decorating.

Florist's wire is essential to secure fruits, bows, and ornaments to greenery. Also use it to make multilooped bows (see "Bows" at right). It comes in foot-long strips; cut it with wire cutters to the size you need.

Wrap the wire end of **florist's picks** around a floral stem and stick the pick end into the greenery.

Paddle wire is stronger than regular florist's wire. Use it to affix garlands and other heavy items to a doorframe.

Florist's sticks are handy to secure greenery to frames.

Hot-glue gun and glue sticks can secure lightweight fruits and ornaments to greenery and topiary forms. Keep an ample supply of glue sticks on hand.

Reserve a sharp pair of scissors to cut only ribbon for cleanly trimmed ends.

Cut wire, florals, and garlands with **wire clippers**. Keep them sharp for decorating.

Measure a mantel, a door frame, or a stairway with **measuring tape** before you decorate it to know how much material is required.

A hammer and nails are essential when hanging a garland over a doorframe.

BOWS *Tying a beautiful bow is a useful skill. With these tips, you'll create showstopping bows all season long.*

EASY AS 1-2-3

Multilooped Bow

For this bow, use 9' of ribbon and a 6" piece of florist's wire. Cut 1' from the ribbon and set it aside.

1. Beginning and ending with 1' tails, fold the remaining ribbon into 6 (1') loops as shown, pinching the ribbon together at the center. Wire the loops in the center to secure.

2. Loosely knot the center of the 1' ribbon. Centering the knot over the wired ribbon, tie the ribbon around the wired loops.

3. Use the wire to attach the bow as desired.

BOW MEASUREMENTS

To make a wreath bow, you need 15' to 18' of #40 ribbon. This makes a generous bow with long tails.

To make ribbon tails to trail a garland or a wreath, estimate one and a half times the length of the area to be covered. This allows for the ribbon ends to be tucked into garlands.

To make a tree, garland, or other accent bow, allow 10' of #40 or #9 ribbon. Add more ribbon for longer tails.

EZ BOW MAKER

The EZ BowMaker is simple to assemble and comes with illustrations that show you step by step how to create beautiful bows.

Use the EZ BowMaker to craft large bows for such things as tree-toppers and wreath bows. You can also make small bows for hair ornaments and packages.

TREE-TRIMMING TIPS
Here are a few hints for hanging lights and decorating with ornaments and garlands.

HOW TO DECORATE WITH GARLANDS AND ORNAMENTS
Enjoy the annual ritual of decorating the tree.

Decorative garlands look fabulous scalloped around the tree. Weave the garland around the tree from the top to the bottom. As a general guide, use 150' of garland for a 9' tree, 100' of garland for a 7½' tree, and 40' of garland for a 4' tree.

To hang the ornaments, put plain glass balls on branches close to the trunk and showcase favorite ornaments near the tip. To secure a heavy ornament, wire it to a tree branch or tie it on with ribbon.

Della Robbia ornaments and bead garland sparkle on a Christmas tree.

HOW TO STRING LIGHTS
Pile on the lights to transform your tree into a spectacular Christmas centerpiece.

To determine how many lights you need, use these numbers as a guideline for moderate coverage: To cover a tree with 100-light strands, use 15 strands for a 9' tree, 12 strands for a 7½' tree, and 7 strands for a 4' tree. If you place the tree against a wall, you may adjust your quantities to put more lights at the front and fewer at the back.

When purchasing lights, make sure that all the strands you buy are compatible and that the wattages are the same. Light strands come in 100-light strands and 50-light strands. Either count will do the job.

Before you begin, plug in each light strand to make sure all lights work. Keep the lights plugged in as you go so that you can see the effect.

As a safety precaution, don't string together more than three strands of lights. Use extension cords that are long enough to reach the plug. Also don't plug more than two extension cords together.

To hang the lights, start at the top of the tree and work your way down. Weave strands of lights in and out of the tree as well as around it, stringing them in toward the trunk and out to the branch tips to create depth.

Take time to step back from the tree occasionally as you string the lights so that you can see any blank spots. It's much easier to fill in those spaces and achieve balance as you go, than to redo the lights at the end.

HOW TO MAKE GREAT GARLANDS
Greet Christmas with rich, thick greenery draped across mantels, curled around doorways, woven through banisters, and highlighted with decorations.

GARLAND MEASUREMENTS

The best way to determine how much garland you need is to measure the item you plan to decorate. These are some average measurements.

Picture-frame swag: 6' (See page 48.)

Stairway: 12' (See page 27.)

Mantel: 18' (See page 44.)

Doorframe: 18' (See page 12.)

Large furniture: 20' (See page 62.)

It took 18' of garland to cover the mantel on page 54, including the puddled ends.

HOW TO EMBELLISH GREENERY

1. To fluff the garland, pull each stem away from the center. Usually it's easier to embellish the greenery before you hang it.

2. For each piece of fruit or ornament you wish to add, run a small piece of florist's wire through it. For picks (not pictured), press the pick into the greenery and secure with wire.

3. Wrap the wire around the greenery and twist the ends together.

4. Once you have added all the embellishments, wrap and tuck the ribbon into the greenery.

INDEX

CONTRIBUTORS

Project Designers

Kim Eidson Crane
Liz Edge
Jan Gautro
Deeya L. Gray
Alisa Jane Hyde
Beth Jordan
L. Victoria Knowles
Duffy Morrison
Cecile Y. Nierodzinski
Catherine Pewitt
Betsy Scott
Carol M. Tipton
Patricia Weaver
Cynthia M. Wheeler

Photography

Keith Harrelson

Homeowners

Carolyn and John Hartman
Susan and Don Huff
Shannon and David Jernigan
Barbara and Ed Randle
Kay and Tom Worley
Linda and Kneeland Wright